The Economics of Information

LIBRARY AND INFORMATION SCIENCE TEXT SERIES

THE ECONOMICS
OF INFORMATION

*A Guide to Economic and Cost-Benefit Analysis
for Information Professionals*

Bruce R. Kingma

1996
LIBRARIES UNLIMITED, INC.
Englewood, Colorado

To my children,
Patrick (running back),
Sabra (power forward), and
George (first baseman).

LIBRARIES UNLIMITED, INC.
P.O. Box 6633
Englewood, CO 80155-6633
1-800-237-6124

Production Editor: Kevin W. Perizzolo
Copy Editor: Tama J. Serfoss
Indexer: Nancy Fulton
Design and Layout: Pamela J. Getchell

Library of Congress Cataloging-in-Publication Data

Kingma, Bruce R.
    The economics of information : a guide to economic and cost-
benefit analysis for information professionals / Bruce R. Kingma.
    xii, 200 p. 17x25 cm. -- (Library and information science text series)
    Includes bibliographical references and index.
    ISBN 1-56308-303-5
    1. Cost effectiveness. 2. Information science--Economic aspects.
3. Economics. 4. Decision-making.   I. Title. II. Series.
HD47.4.K56   1996
658.15'54--dc20   95-48861
                                                                  CIP

Contents

Part I
An Introduction to Economics

Part II
Market Failure and Information Markets

Part III
An Introduction to Cost-Benefit Analysis

Preface

Students earning their Masters of Business Administration, Masters of Public Administration, and Masters of Nonprofit Management degrees are required to take a class in economics. However, only a handful of students in Masters of Library Science and Masters of Information Science programs study economics. This is unfortunate because many individuals with M.L.S. or M.I.S. degrees become information managers, library directors, and information policymakers, positions that require a working knowledge of the economics of information. This book is written to make up that deficiency, offering an introduction to economics for librarians and information professionals. In each chapter, basic economic concepts—demand, supply, benefits, costs—are presented, illustrated with examples of the goods and services of information markets.

This book, written by an economist, provides readers with an introduction to economics and cost-benefit analysis and will be particularly valuable to individuals who are, or hope to be, managers of information services in academic, public, or special libraries. It will also be useful to those with no background in economics who plan to research the value and cost of information. The economic tools presented will help information managers and policymakers make better decisions. After completing this book, readers will have a better understanding of information markets, be able to understand economic research on information topics, and have the skills to complete basic cost-benefit analyses of information goods and services.

The Economics of Information evolved over the past five years from my lecture notes for "The Economics of Information Management" class in the M.L.S., M.I.S., and Ph.D. programs at the School of Information Science and Policy at the State University of New York at Albany. It is also developed in part from personal experience, extensive discussions with professional colleagues, and a thorough review of the professional literature. While the economics of information continues to be one of the most controversial and popular topics for research in information science, this class is one of only a handful of economics classes taught in information science programs.[1]

The focus of this book is on the economics of information goods and services, which are sufficiently different from other types of goods and services that a complete understanding of their differences is important to information managers and policymakers. For example, information affects individuals other than those who directly consume and produce it. Print or broadcast news can be shared by many individuals without decreasing its value or worth. Information goods and services frequently have high fixed costs of production and lower marginal costs of reproduction. In addition, copyright and patent laws protect the original owner of intellectual property and establish the owner as the single supplier, or monopolist, of the information. Finally, those with specialized information, such as mechanics or doctors, can exploit those without such information by misrepresenting quality and costs, thereby creating an incentive for information markets about the quality of goods and services to be performed. Each of these characteristics of information is important in developing cost-benefit models of information goods and services.

This book is divided into three parts and 13 chapters. Part I, which includes chapters 1 through 4, provides an introduction to economic analysis. Chapter 1 is an introduction to economics as a science and a method of analysis. This chapter also discusses the difference between economic costs and accounting costs. Chapter 2 introduces the reader to consumer theory and the concept of *demand* and shows how to measure the benefits from consumption. Chapter 3 describes *supply* theory and demonstrates how to measure the costs of production. Chapter 4 combines the theories of demand and supply to analyze how market price and quantity are chosen and introduces the notion of economic or socially efficient markets.

Part II, chapters 5 through 9, defines *market failure*, in which information markets fail to operate efficiently. Chapter 5 discusses *externalities*—costs or benefits incurred by individuals who are not direct consumers or producers of the good. Chapter 6 presents models of information as a public good shared by many consumers simultaneously. Modeling information as a public good requires a collective method of finance, in which all consumers of the good pay their fair share to cover its costs. In chapter 7, noncompetitive information markets, in which the seller of the information good or service is the sole provider and can charge prices sufficiently above costs to prevent the market from achieving economic efficiency, are presented. These noncompetitive information markets can be the result of copyright or patent laws that assign exclusive ownership. Chapter 8 describes the problems of imperfect information—in which either consumers or producers or both do not fully understand the quality of a good. This chapter then goes on to demonstrate the need for information to correct this market failure. Chapter 9 compares economic models of information as a commodity with models of information as a public good.

Part III, including chapters 10 through 13, provides an introduction to the tools of cost-benefit analysis. Chapter 10 examines user fees in information markets. The economics of user fees for libraries and information services, while controversial, has never been fully explained in information science literature. Chapter 11 describes how economics can be used to measure "time spent" and how the value of information services includes the time spent waiting for information to be delivered. Quantifying the value of time enables a more accurate calculation of the benefits from reference services, interlibrary loan, and computer usage. Chapter 12 analyzes resource-sharing, such as occurs in interlibrary loan among libraries. Chapter 13 concludes this book by providing the reader with the tools to conduct a cost-benefit analysis. This includes setting up a matrix of major stakeholders for any management or policy decision, and measuring the benefits and costs to each stakeholder group.

The economic concepts described in this book are not new; however, the application of these tools to the information markets presented in this book is new. For a more detailed discussion of the economic terms and concepts presented in this book, the reader may want to consult the undergraduate economics text by Samuelson and Nordaus (1995) or the graduate economics text by Becker (1971).[2] The reader may also be interested in texts by Van House (1983), Getz (1980), Schauer (1986), Cronin and Davenport (1991), Cummings, et al. (1992), Smith (1991), Griffiths and King (1993), and Kraft and Boyce (1991), all of which analyze library services using many of the economic, accounting, and management concepts presented here.[3] This book complements these texts by presenting and applying economic theory to several markets for information goods and services including library services.

A number of people helped me in writing this book, including my students in the Economics of Information class at the University at Albany, State University of New York. Deborah Andersen, Steven Black, Jean Galbraith, and Steven Shadle were particularly helpful. I would also like to thank George Chressanthis, Thomas Galvin, and an anonymous reader for helpful comments. Beth Bruder at Case Western Reserve University helped with the diagrams, and Lisa Mullenneaux, Rita Ganguly, and Donna LaHue reviewed the manuscript.

Notes

1. See Terry L. Weech, "The Teaching of Economics of Information in Schools of Library and Information Science in the U.S.—A Preliminary Analysis," *American Society for Information Science Conference Proceedings* 30 (1994): 70-75; and Terry L. Weech, "The Economics of Information and the Professional Training of Librarians and Information Scientists in the United States," *Economics of Information: Conference Proceedings* (Lyon, France: ENSSIB, 1995).

2. Paul A. Samuelson and William D. Nordaus, *Economics*, 15th ed. (New York: McGraw-Hill, 1995); and Gary S. Becker, *Economic Theory* (New York: Knopf, 1971).

3.   Nancy A. Van House, *Public Library User Fees: The Use and Finance of Public Libraries* (Westport, CT: Greenwood, 1983). Malcolm Getz, *Public Libraries: An Economic View* (Baltimore: Johns Hopkins University Press, 1980). Bruce P. Schauer, *The Economics of Managing Library Service* (Chicago: American Library Association, 1986). Blaise Cronin and Elisabeth Davenport, *Elements of Information Management* (Metuchen, NJ: Scarecrow Press, 1991). Anthony M. Cummings, Marcia L. Witte, William G. Bowen, Laura O. Lazarus, and Richard H. Ekman, *University Libraries and Scholarly Communications* (Washington, DC: Association of Research Libraries for the Andrew W. Mellon Foundation, 1992). G. Stevenson Smith, *Managerial Accounting for Libraries and Other Not-For-Profit Organizations* (Chicago: American Library Association, 1991). Jose-Marie Griffiths and Donald W. King, *Special Libraries: Increasing the Information Edge* (Washington, DC: Special Libraries Association, 1993). Donald H. Kraft and Bert R. Boyce, *Operations Research for Libraries and Information Agencies: Techniques for the Evaluation of Management Decision Alternatives* (San Diego: Academic Press, 1991).

An Introduction to Economics

Introduction

Information managers make policy decisions every day. Each decision is a choice among competing alternatives. For example, a library director must choose how to allocate a $1,000,000 budget among staff, supplies, books, and other expenditures. Thus, the decision to open the library on Sundays may mean that money cannot be spent to buy books and computers or to increase reference staff hours during the week. A corporate information resources manager may have to decide which photocopy machine to buy based on the staff's needs and available funds. Even in one's personal life, one must decide how to spend time and money from among a set of alternatives: to see a movie or rent a videotape; to write a letter, use electronic mail, or make a telephone call.

As a science, economics examines how these decisions are made and which alternative provides the greatest benefit to the various *stakeholders*, people or groups with an interest in the decision. Economics also provides a set of research tools—demand, supply, costs, benefits—to analyze these decisions. These tools enable managers and policymakers to quantify the benefits and costs for each stakeholder and make "economically efficient" decisions.

Economics is defined as the study of the allocation of scarce resources. Examples of scarce resources include: a library budget, personal income, or the federal budget. Scarce resources can also mean land, employees, time, books, computers, gigabits, electromagnetic spectrum or airwaves, or fiber-optic capacity. In each example, there exists a limited amount of something to be consumed or used in producing a good or service. Allocating these scarce resources means determining how to use, spend, or divide the resources, in other words, how to spend the library budget, how to allocate hard disk space to store computer files, how to schedule employees' time, how to allocate the electromagnetic spectrum or airwaves, or how to manage personal time. In each case, choices have to be made to make the best use of limited resources.

Each alternative use of a scarce resource benefits various stakeholders, which the economist quantifies. For example, given the different ways in which a library budget can be allocated, the economist can attempt to measure the benefits provided to patrons, librarians, and the community in the case of a public library or the company in the case of a corporate library. Alternatively, the economist can attempt to measure which among an array of information products—computers, video, print—provides the greatest benefit to consumers on limited budgets.

Why Study Economics?

Economics enables us to analyze management and policy choices. For example, suppose a library director needs to determine how best to spend $100,000 the library received this year in additional funding from the state. Should she hire an additional employee, purchase more books, purchase more computer equipment, or choose some combination of these three? What guidelines should she follow to make these decisions?

Or suppose the corporate information resource manager must allocate five new computers among 10 employees. Who should get a new computer? Should he give the new computers to the employees with the oldest computers, the employees with the most seniority, or use some other rule to allocate the computers?

Finally, suppose a foundation grants officer is responsible for distributing $1,000,000 in grants to schools, libraries, and nonprofit organizations who have submitted proposals outlining how they would use the money to take advantage of the information superhighway. Should the grants officer give the money to organizations serving the neediest populations, those with the greatest likelihood of success with their projects, those with the greatest financial stability, or those with the least financial stability?

Economics—or more specifically cost-benefit analysis—provides a set of theoretical and empirical tools necessary to make the best choices in each of these circumstances. In each case, the manager, director, or policymaker must weigh the costs and benefits of each alternative to each stakeholder. If the benefits of an alternative exceed the costs, it is an *economically efficient* alternative. Options that provide the greatest net benefit are the most economically efficient options. If the costs exceed the benefits, it is an *economically inefficient* alternative.

Economics is not the only way to evaluate management and policy decisions; however, economics provides an unbiased, objective method of analysis. Economists avoid such value statements as "a clean environment is good" or "there should be a free flow of and open access to government information." Instead economists use a ledger of costs and benefits for each possible decision, choosing through those means the most economically efficient alternative.

For example, we know that a clean environment provides many health benefits. However, the costs of a clean environment include catalytic converters for automobiles and chemical smokestack "scrubbers" for factories. If the benefits can be quantified and if they exceed the costs, an economist can prove that it is economically efficient to support a clean environment. In another example, open access to government information provides the benefit of an informed electorate. This benefit may take the form of preventing poor policy making by elected officials or of enabling the electorate to more easily identify incompetent officials. The costs of open access to government information include the costs of storing, cataloging, and reproducing government documents. Open access to government documents might also reveal state secrets, jeopardizing national security, or might reveal personal secrets, harming or embarrassing individuals and violating their rights to privacy. Therefore, for reasons of national security or personal privacy, access to government information may need to be restricted. An economic analysis of open access to government documents weighs the benefits that citizens receive from such access against the costs of providing that access for different categories of documents.

Economics is more than accounting. Accounting provides the numbers necessary for cost-benefit analysis, but does not provide the tools of analysis. Managerial accounting—which includes break-even analysis, cost analysis, and performance analysis—provides some of the tools to analyze costs. However, economics provides additional tools such as the concepts of demand, marginal benefit, and consumer surplus, and the cost-analysis tools of supply, marginal cost, and producer surplus, enabling managers and policymakers to decide how to spend a budget, implement a policy, or provide a good or service.

Consumers enjoy identifiable benefits from the use of goods and services while producers spend identifiable costs on the production of a good or provision of a service. When a library director considers keeping the library open an extra hour, he weighs the costs of staff and utilities to the benefits patrons might receive. When a publisher considers launching another journal title, she weighs the costs of editing, typesetting, and printing to the revenues received from sales. When policymakers consider imposing access regulations to the information superhighway, they weigh the costs to taxpayers and groups who may have to pay to use the information superhighway or may be denied access to it to the benefits to those groups that may receive increased access. In each example, economics and cost-benefit analysis give us the tools to analyze these alternatives, quantify the benefits and costs, and determine the most economically efficient choice.

Examples throughout this book demonstrate the usefulness of economic analysis in management and policy decisions. In most of these examples, the economic models are explained using fictitious numbers to give the reader the calculations behind the cost-benefit analysis. Cost-benefit analyses of information markets presented here include telephone directory assistance, academic library journal subscription policies, government policy on sex education, junk mail legislation, access to the information superhighway, copyright and patent law, journal pricing, and book publishing.

Why Study the Economics of Information?

Managers and policymakers are increasingly confronted by economic choices involving information goods and services—computer resources, journals, software, and records, including electronic records. Furthermore, the purchase of these goods and services have far-reaching effects. Purchasing a local area network (LAN) that connects all computer workstations within an organization, for example, will influence the communications, teamwork, and ultimately productivity of the entire organization. Decisions about whether to purchase photocopiers, long-distance services, fax machines, or software and hardware and whether to hire technical and systems support personnel, reference staff, and librarians are critical in an organization because, while the costs of these products, services, or personnel may or may not be a significant part of the organization's budget, their impact on organization productivity can be considerable. Advertisements for a popular overnight delivery service show a manager losing his job as a result of choosing the wrong service. Usually such low-cost decisions— less than $20—do not have such drastic consequences. What these commercials do emphasize is that the consequences of an information management decision can be greater than its cost.

Policymakers are also confronted with increasingly difficult choices because policy issues are more complex in an electronic environment. With current technology, corporate and personal records can be easily copied, which may affect productivity and personal well-being. Additionally, while the lower transaction costs and increased accessibility of information in electronic format may improve corporate productivity, it may also decrease productivity by removing the economic incentive to produce as other firms can more easily copy and imitate a new product. Similarly, while electronic records may open credit markets more quickly to individuals with excellent credit history, they may also make it easier for employers, credit collectors, government agencies, and others to access private, personal information. The need for revised Internet regulations, copyright and patent laws, and tele-communications regulations as well as consideration of the privacy of personal records and other information policy issues are heightened by the ease of recording, reproduction, access, and transfer of information through electronic technology.

Why Is Information Economics Different?

Most economists believe that competitive markets unfettered by government regulation usually achieve efficient levels of production and consumption for most goods and services. This does not mean, however, that everyone gets everything they want. It means that given the resources available, the competitive market's "invisible hand" allocates goods and services to achieve what economists call a *pareto optimum*. A pareto optimum is an allocation of production and consumption such that no one can be made better off without making someone else worse off.

Sometimes, though, competitive markets do not efficiently allocate information goods and services. When this happens there is a *market failure*, in which the market fails to make an efficient allocation, suggesting that government intervention may be necessary to improve economic efficiency. For example, copyright and patent laws were passed to correct a market that, in the absence of these laws, would never achieve a level of output that would benefit the most people. Without copyright law, the intellectual property of authors would not be protected and, as a result, authors might not receive sufficient compensation for their work, compensation that provides incentive for authors and inventors to pursue creative endeavors. Copyright law protects the author's ownership of his work and thereby provides an incentive for future creative authorship.

Market failure for information goods and services occurs for several reasons. In the case of intellectual property, the cost of reproducing a work is usually much lower than the cost of purchasing the original. For example, it is usually less expensive to make an illegal copy of a copyrighted software program than to purchase a legal copy from the software vendor, because the cost of illegally copying material doesn't include compensation for the author or inventor. This is the result of the *public good* or *commons* nature of intellectual property (a public good is a product or service that can be used by many consumers either simultaneously or over a period of time) and results in a market failure, in which the producer of a good or service is not fairly compensated for the product and therefore has no incentive to continue producing. The risk of this kind of market failure justifies intellectual property protection by copyright, patent, and trade secret laws.

However, protecting intellectual property through laws results in the author or publisher being a *monopolist,* or sole owner of a good, and can result in another form of market failure. To maximize profits from the sale of the intellectual property, the monopolist copyright owner increases the price of that property to the public. The market failure occurs if the monopolist's price, the cost to the consumer, exceeds the benefit that some consumers will receive from the good. As a result many consumers will be prevented from purchasing the good or service, even though the benefit that they would receive from it exceeds the costs of providing the good or service, thereby decreasing economic efficiency.

In general, competitive markets operate efficiently because of the voluntary exchange between consumers and producers. In a normal competitive market, if a producer prices a good or service so that the cost outweighs the benefits to the consumers, lack of sales will soon force a price reduction. On the other hand, consumers will be willing to pay more for a good or service of proven benefits, allowing producers to raise prices accordingly. However, the decisions of those purchasing or selling goods and services in information markets frequently affect individuals other than consumers and producers. If, for example, a direct marketing firm purchases the services of the mail or telephone company, individuals who receive junk mail or telephone solicitations are not voluntarily purchasing these solicitations. The 'cost' of reading and disposing of the mail or answering the phone is an *externality—* cost or benefit incurred by individuals who are not direct consumers or producers of the good—imposed on them by the direct marketing firm.

Finally, competitive markets operate efficiently only when consumers and producers have full information about the quality of their purchases and sales. Information markets arise to correct the market inefficiencies caused by *imperfect information* that affects consumer and producer choices. Consumer product magazines, medical and legal journals, private investigators, and environmental watchdog groups are all examples of production designed to correct problems of imperfect information in existing markets.

The economics of information goods and services requires managers, policymakers, and economists to think carefully about their choices, policies, and analyses. Economic analysis of information goods and services is different from standard economic analysis. While this book uses standard microeconomic theory as a foundation for examining these markets, it also defines the peculiarities of the economics of information goods and services.

Economics as a Science

Economists use mathematics to quantify the benefits and costs of decisions and make unbiased, scientific assessments of value. Sometimes a manager's perception of the benefits and costs is enough to make the right decision even though these benefits and costs have not been explicitly measured. For example, if the library budget for collection development increases, it may be enough for the acquisition librarian to subscribe to the additional journals she feels will best serve the library based on the opinions of a few patrons who have requested those journal titles. In this case, it may be relatively simple to determine which journals to purchase. The librarian simply assumes that the value to the patrons of requested journals exceeds the value of other journals for which no requests have been made.

At other times, it is important to explicitly calculate the benefits and costs of a policy or management decision; however, quantifying those costs and benefits can be difficult. For example, if the government provided telephone service to everyone in the country who could not afford it, the costs would be easily measured by adding up the cost of local phone service and installation for each of these households.

The benefit from universal phone service is more difficult to calculate. Individuals who are too poor to pay for a telephone would benefit from communications access previously unavailable to them. Those who can afford a telephone would also benefit by having telephone access to more individuals than before. Schools would now have access to the parents of all pupils; government agencies would now have access to more clients; businesses would have access to more potential consumers; and all household would have immediate access to emergency services. However, it is difficult to quantify or measure these benefits. And yet, to presume that universal telephone service is a worthwhile objective is to presume that these benefits are greater than the costs.

Economics, as a science, would attempt to quantify the benefits and costs of universal telephone service without prejudging whether such an objective is "good" or "bad." Rather than taking sides in the debate of whether telephone or other information services are a fundamental right or whether those services should only go to those who pay for them, the science of economics simply determines if there is a net benefit from a policy. Of course, the measurement of benefits and costs may be debatable depending on the individual economist's view of what items belong on which side of the ledger, the relative value placed on each benefit, and the underlying assumptions of the economic model. However, all economists use the same set of economic tools—demand, supply, marginal cost, marginal benefit—to make their calculations.

Economics is also the study of human behavior. The cornerstone of economic models of human behavior is the assumption that individuals behave rationally in ways they believe give them the most net benefit. Everyone goes through life facing choices—Should I become a fireman or a librarian? Should I purchase a new car or fix the old one? Should I read a novel or watch television?—and each individual makes a set of choices based on what they believe will provide them with the most benefit. Tom may decide to have his old car fixed rather than purchase a new car because he expects that the repairs will cost less and last a sufficient period of time to get the maximum net benefit from the old car. Additionally, Tom may not have the savings to purchase a new car, or he may simply have a nostalgic attachment to the old car. Economics is used to explain human behavior based on the rational choices of individuals acting in their own self-interest.

Given the assumption of rational behavior, economic tools have proven remarkably useful and reliable in studying, not only traditional markets, but also such diverse information markets as drugs, crime, marriage, fertility, charity, and religion. For example, fertility among teenagers is related to teenage perceptions of the probability of pregnancy, standards of living, education, job opportunities, and sex education. A teenager considering having sexual relations is making a fundamentally economic choice, comparing the benefits of his or her action with the potential costs of pregnancy, disease, and reputation. Accurate information provided at home or at school may influence a teenager's perception of the risks or costs associated with sexual relations and therefore may decrease the number of unwanted pregnancies.[1]

Another arena in which people make economic choices is the marriage market. Courtship is the process of collecting information on the likelihood of a beneficial match between oneself and another. Marriage is a legal agreement in which both parties agree to stop collecting information on other potential mates. Divorce is the acknowledgment by one or both parties that incomplete information was collected during courtship.[2] Similarly, the market for religion is a market for information. Religious leaders must convince their congregations that they have a set of religious beliefs that will lead to salvation. Each religious leader "sells" to their congregations the information they have about salvation.[3]

The science of economics uses theories and models of costs and benefits to explain and examine human behavior. Any action by a manager, policymaker, patron, or client will result in costs and benefits to a set of stakeholders. Customers purchase goods because they believe the benefits from those purchases will outweigh the costs, while suppliers believe the revenue they receive will outweigh the costs of providing those goods. Economics, as a science, uses the theories of consumer behavior (*demand*) and producer behavior (*supply*) to explain market transactions.

Accounting Costs and Opportunity Costs

One of the most important tools that economic models offer to managers and policymakers is the notion of the *opportunity cost* of a good or service, the highest value of alternative opportunities foregone by consuming a good or service. Opportunity costs differ from financial or monetary costs because they include not only the money spent purchasing a good, but also the value of time spent, promises made, and opportunities lost when a good or service is consumed. For example, the opportunity cost of going to see a movie is the price of the movie ticket plus the value of the time spent watching the movie. If instead of seeing the movie, the individual reads the book on which the movie is based, the opportunity cost is the price of the book plus the value of the time spent reading the book. Even if a good does not have a monetary cost, it may still have an opportunity cost. A book borrowed from the library does not have a monetary cost to the patron but does have an opportunity cost of acquiring and reading it.

Economists use the opportunity costs of goods and services to represent the full or actual cost of consumption or purchases. The opportunity cost of watching the evening news is the value of the time spent watching it. The time spent watching the news cannot be used on some other activity. For example, instead of watching the news on television you may choose to listen to the news on the radio and repair your car at the same time, essentially getting the information at a lower opportunity cost. However, you might also enjoy relaxing and watching the news on television. If this is the case, watching the news, even at a higher opportunity cost, might still provide you with a greater benefit than listening to it.

In any cost-benefit analysis the analyst must be concerned with the opportunity cost of all alternatives to determine economically efficient management or policy decisions. Using only the financial cost for management decisions will result in economic costs being under-estimated and may, therefore, lead to decisions that decrease economic efficiency.

An obvious example of the importance of opportunity costs are the management decisions made within every library's interlibrary loan office. An interlibrary loan librarian may have two alternative sources for a research article: the article may be ordered from a commercial delivery service or it may be ordered from another library. Suppose the commercial delivery service could deliver the article in two days at a cost of $20. The library would take one week but delivery would be free. The accounting or financial cost difference between these two services would suggest that the article should be ordered from the library; however, there is an opportunity cost of an additional five days to the patron of waiting for the article. For the patron, the value of early access to the article may outweigh the financial cost difference.

While the value of time is the most frequently cited difference between accounting and opportunity costs, opportunity costs are more broadly defined as the highest value of foregone opportunities. Making a choice implies that alternative opportunities are foregone. For example, the opportunity cost of lending a book to someone is the cost of not being able to access the information in it. The opportunity cost of occupying a seat at a popular lecture is the value of that seat to someone else who may not be able to attend if all the seats are filled. The opportunity cost of someone using one among a limited number of compact disk workstations at the library is the value to the next person of using that workstation. While in each example the financial cost is zero, there is an opportunity cost.

Opportunity costs also include the cost of foregone opportunities by the entrepreneur, investor, researcher, and anyone else who pursues one of several alternatives, foregoing the opportunity to gain profit or knowledge from something else. For example, the economic cost of producing books by the owner of a publishing firm includes the financial cost of paper, print, and labor plus the opportunity cost of the salary the publisher could have earned had she pursued another profession plus the opportunity cost of any financial investment the publisher may have in the firm. The publisher may have previously worked for another publishing firm and earned $50,000 per year. In addition to foregoing her salary, this entrepreneurial publisher may have invested $100,000 in establishing her own publishing firm. The opportunity cost of this investment is the amount of interest the publisher would have received had the money been placed in a risk-free savings account instead. Therefore, in addition to at least $50,000 per year in salary, assuming an interest rate of 5 percent, this publisher has foregone at least $5,000 per year in interest income. Other examples of economic costs include the researcher who spends a year on one project and forgoes the value of other discoveries that could have been made during that year, and the student who skips class and forgoes the value of the lecture.

Because there is no price or charge associated with economic costs, they are more difficult to calculate than accounting costs but they are important in making efficient policy and management decisions. Therefore, throughout this book the distinction between economic or opportunity costs and financial, monetary, or accounting costs is stressed.[4]

Summary

Managers and policy analysts choose among competing alternatives for every decision they make. Economics enables the manager and policy analyst to make better, more informed decisions about these choices by identifying their costs and benefits. Economics, as a science, quantifies the value of costs and benefits to determine the most economically efficient alternatives.

Economic analysis uses demand, supply, cost-benefit analysis, opportunity costs, and other tools to improve management and policy decisions. This book examines economic theories and shows how they apply to specific examples of information markets.

Information economics applies the tools of economic analysis to information goods and services. Information goods and services have characteristics that often result in market failure, such as problems of imperfect information, public goods, and noncompetitive markets requiring policy intervention to ensure economic efficiency. Managers also need a complete understanding of the economics of information to accurately calculate the costs and benefits of information goods and services.

Discussion Questions

1. List the stakeholders in each of the following examples:

    *   A company must allocate five new computers among 10 employees.

    *   A library must purchase a new photocopy machine from one of several potential vendors.

    *   The National Science Foundation must award 10 grants on research related to Internet access by elementary school students.

2. For each stakeholder, discuss the costs and benefits of the alternatives.

3. In each of the following examples, how does the acquisition of information influence the market? How do providers of these goods or services use information or disinformation to facilitate the consumer's choice? How might someone try to counteract disinformation?

    *   You must purchase a new car.

    *   A burglar must decide which home to rob.

- You have decided to give $100 to charity, but must decide which nonprofit organization to give it to.

- You have decided to start attending religious services, but must decide which services—for example, Jewish, Catholic, Protestant, Muslim, or other—to attend.

4. Assume you are the director of a public library and are given the following assessment of the costs and benefits of three photocopiers that can be purchased. Assume the library needs only one photocopier and has the funds to purchase any one of the three. Which machine should you purchase? Why?

Machine	Estimated Benefit	Estimated Cost
A	$ 5,000	$2,000
B	$10,000	$3,700
C	$12,000	$6,000

5. Describe the financial costs and opportunity costs of each of the following services: interlibrary loan, book borrowing from the library, purchasing a book from a store, renting a videotape, searching a database for information on a research topic.

Notes

1. See Gary S. Becker, *A Treatise on the Family* (Cambridge, MA: Harvard University Press, 1991).

2. For additional reading on marriage markets see Elizabeth Peters, "Marriage and Divorce: Informational Constraints and Private Contracting," *American Economic Review* (1986): 237-54.

3. For additional reading on religious markets see Laurence R. Iannaccone, "Sacrifice and Stigma: Reducing Free-Riding in Cults, Communes, and Other Collectives," *Journal of Political Economy* 100, no. 2 (1992): 271-91; and Laurence R. Iannaccone, "The Consequences of Religious Market Structure: Adam Smith and the Economics of Religion," paper in Political Economy Report, University of Western Ontario, 1991.

4. For additional examples of opportunity costs see Robert E. Bickner, "Concepts of Economic Cost," *Cost Considerations in Systems Analysis*, ed. Gene H. Fisher (New York: American Elsevier, 1971), 24-63; and Richard B. McKenzie, "The Economist's Paradigm," *Library Trends* 28, no. 1 (Summer 1979): 7-24.

Consumer Theory and Market Demand

2

Whenever you buy a book, magazine, newspaper, or a computer program; make a telephone call; rent a video; or buy a movie ticket, you are expressing a *demand* for that good or service, the amount of the good you are willing and able to purchase in a given period of time. This year, you may buy 10 books, 100 newspapers, two computer programs, and 50 hours of long-distance phone calls. Your purchase of these goods shows your willingness to pay for them. The *market demand* for a good or service is the sum of the quantity demanded by all individual consumers. *Consumer theory* explains the factors that influence the decisions of consumers to purchase goods and services.

Each consumer makes a decision about how much of a good or service to purchase based on the price, their level of income, the prices of similar goods, and their tastes or preferences for a particular good or service. Consumer theory explains how to quantify or measure these factors to predict how a change in any one factor will influence the quantity demanded. For example, if the price per minute of a long-distance phone call were to increase from $1 to $1.50, you might decrease the amount of time you spend on the phone or decrease the number of phone calls you make. In addition, you might disconnect your teenager's telephone and purchase more stamps for letters. Each of these decisions is an expression of a change in the quantity of long-distance phone service demanded as a result of a change in the price of long-distance service. Likewise, if your income were to increase by 20 percent, or the price of a first-class stamp were to increase to $0.50, or if you were to move to another state, your demand for long-distance phone service would likely change. These changes are predicted and measured by consumer theory.

Consumer Theory and the Demand for Books

There are five factors that influence the demand for a good or service: the price of the good, consumer income, the prices of related goods, consumer tastes, and the number of potential consumers. Of these five factors, the price of the good is the most studied because it connects the consumers of a good with the suppliers or producers of it. Consumers pay a price that producers or sellers receive as revenue. The price serves as a mechanism of exchange between producers and consumers. The price provides information to producers and consumers about the cost and value of the goods and services being exchanged.

The Price Effect

The relationship between the price of a good and the quantity demanded is expressed in the *law of demand*, which states that there is an inverse relationship between the price a consumer pays for a good and the quantity demanded, holding all else constant. If the price increases, consumers will decrease the amount purchased of a good. If the price decreases consumers will increase their purchases of a good. The law of demand holds for individual consumers as well as the market.

Table 2.1 illustrates the law of demand, showing the results of a simple, hypothetical, market survey of three individuals—Patrick, Sabra, and George—who are potential buyers of books on the Civil War. The demand for new books on the Civil War by Patrick, Sabra, and George in a year is the number of books they are willing to purchase at a given price.

Table 2.1.
The Demand for Books

Number of Books Purchased					
Price	Patrick	Sabra	George	All Others	Market Demand
$50	1	0	0	10,999	11,000
$45	2	1	0	12,997	13,000
$40	3	2	1	14,994	15,000
$35	4	3	2	16,991	17,000
$30	5	4	3	18,988	19,000

According to table 2.1, if the price of a Civil War book is $50, Patrick will purchase one book a year; Sabra and George will not purchase any. If the price of new books on the Civil War falls to $45—holding the quality of books constant—Patrick will increase his purchases of books to two per year, and Sabra will increase her purchases to one per year. For either Patrick or Sabra to purchase more books, the price will have to fall below $45. However, consumers such as George are only willing to purchase books on the Civil War when the price falls to $40 or less.

The market demand for a good is the sum of the individual demand by each consumer. Table 2.1 shows that as the price falls from $50 to $45, annual sales increase from 11,000 to 13,000 books. The increase in the market demand is the sum of the increase in purchases by existing consumers plus additional purchases by new consumers. In table 2.1, as the price falls from $45 to $40 Patrick and Sabra increase the number of books they purchase, while George enters the market as a new consumer.

A demand curve is a graph of the relationship between price and quantity for an individual consumer or a market. Figure 2.1 and figure 2.2 illustrate Patrick's demand curve and the market demand curve for new books on the Civil War. Figures 2.1 and 2.2 show that at a given price, there is a unique quantity of Civil War books purchased by Patrick and in the market in a year. Using the demand curve and given the average price of a Civil War book, the number of Civil War books sold this year can be determined.

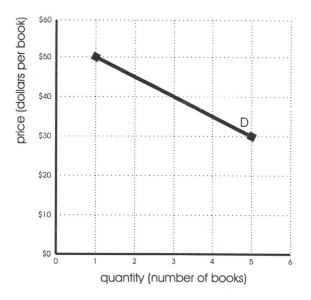

Figure 2.1. Patrick's Demand for Books in Relationship to Price.

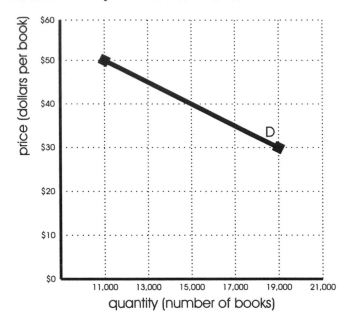

Figure 2.2. Market Demand for Books in Relationship to Price.

Patrick's purchases, as part of the market demand, can be identified in figure 2.2. The first book sold to Patrick is the 11,000th book sold in the market. The second book sold to Patrick is the 13,000th book sold in the market. Each individual consumer's purchase of a book, as part of the market demand for books, is a point on the demand curve in figure 2.2.

Similar market demand curves can be created for every good and service. Producers and suppliers engage in extensive market analysis of goods and services to measure the market demand for their products and to measure the influence of factors other than price on consumer demand for products. The other factors that influence the quantity demanded of a good are consumer income, tastes, and the prices of similar or related goods.

The Income Effect

For most goods and services, as income increases, the demand for that good increases. These goods are called *normal* goods. For a normal good, as income increases, the individual and market demand curves shift to the right such that at all price levels consumers are willing to purchase more. This effect is illustrated in figures 2.3 and 2.4.

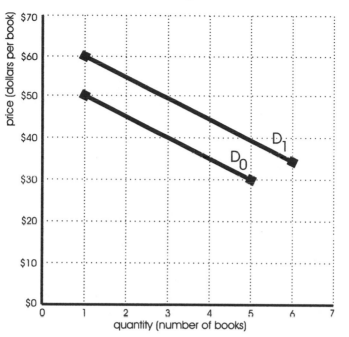

Figure 2.3. Patrick's Demand for Books as Income Increases.

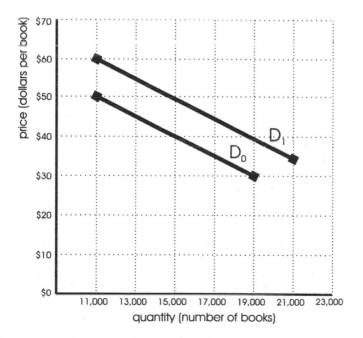

Figure 2.4. Market Demand for Books as Income Increases.

As Patrick's income increases from \$30,000 per year to \$31,000 per year, his demand for Civil War books increases from D_0 to D_1 (see fig. 2.3). If the average price of books on the Civil War is \$40, Patrick's annual purchases will increase from three to four books a year. If the average income of consumers of Civil War books increases from \$30,000 to \$31,000, the demand increases from D_0 to D_1 (see fig. 2.4). At an average price of \$40 per book, the market purchases of Civil War books will increase from 15,000 to 16,000 books per year.

For some goods, as income increases the demand for that good decreases. These are called *inferior* goods. Typically these goods are low quality or generic substitutes for higher quality goods. For example, used books on the Civil War, a low-speed computer, and re-built telephones might all be examples of inferior goods. In these cases, as income increases, consumers begin to purchase the higher quality goods rather than their inferior substitutes, causing the demand for the inferior good to fall.

An income effect can also be the result of a change in price of a single good or service that results in a dramatic increase or decrease in income and therefore a change in the consumption of other goods. An example of this is the rise in the price of scholarly journals for academic libraries. As the prices of scholarly journals rise, academic libraries cut back not only on journal subscriptions but also on monographs. The decline in monograph expenditures was the result of an income effect for the academic library.

Several studies have measured the income effect for information-related goods and services. For example, Kingma (1989) demonstrated that donors increase their contributions to public radio by \$0.54 for every \$1,000 increase in income.[1]

The Prices of Related Goods and Services

Related goods are goods such as *substitute* goods, which consumers might purchase instead of a particular good, or *complement* goods, which consumers might purchase in combination with or as the result of another purchase. For example, substitute goods for new hardcover books on the Civil War might include used or paperback books on the Civil War. The price of a substitute good or service is directly related to the demand for the original good or service. If the average price of a paperback book on the Civil War were to decrease from \$12 to \$10, a corresponding decrease would be seen in the demand for new hardcover books on the Civil War as consumers choose to purchase paperback books instead of hardcover.

The substitute for a journal subscription or book purchase is to borrow the journal or book from the library. Likewise, the academic library's substitute for a journal subscription is to provide access to the information via interlibrary loan. Haley and Talaga (1992) showed that as subscription prices of research journals have escalated, academic libraries have increased access to these titles via interlibrary loan.[2]

The price of a complement good is inversely related to the demand for the original good. Civil War memorabilia or videotapes on the Civil War are complements to new books on the Civil War. If the average price of the videotapes of the PBS series on the Civil War decreased from $150 to $50, consumers of the video series might be more interested in reading books on the Civil War, which would increase the demand for new books on the Civil War. The use of bibliographic indexes on compact disks to search journal articles in an academic library and the requests for these articles from interlibrary loan; pencils and paper; and computers and floppy disks are all examples of complementary goods.

Number of Consumers, Consumer Tastes, and Preferences

The final two variables that influence the quantity demanded are the number of consumers and consumer tastes. As the number of consumers increases, the demand for Civil War books increases. The number of consumers may increase from an increase in the population, or from the publisher expanding into foreign markets that it previously did not sell in.

Unexplained variations in demand for a good are usually considered to represent changes in consumer tastes. For example, consumers who did not view the PBS series on the Civil War might find that their friends, neighbors, and coworkers are spending more time conversing about the Civil War. These consumers may increase their demand for Civil War books to be able to join in on these conversations. However, it cannot be demonstrated that the consumption of the PBS series influenced the increased demand for Civil War books. Rather, the increase in demand should be described as a change in consumer tastes for books on the Civil War.

Increased use of the Internet can be considered a change in tastes for the information services and goods available on the information superhighway. The technology has made a service accessible that was incomprehensible 10 years ago.

The Price Elasticity of Demand

The influence of these five factors (price, income, prices of related goods, consumer tastes, and the number of potential consumers) on the demand for a good or service can be measured using data on the quantity of a good or service purchased, consumers' levels of income, and prices of related goods over time. A publisher might use a telephone survey of individuals who have purchased books in the past, or who own book-buyers' cards, to get information on consumer income, related purchases, and the type and quantity of books purchased. Previous store sales, book prices, number of store customers, store location, and other information is used by book sellers to estimate the demand for books in general and in individual categories such as computer books, textbooks, and children's books. Publishers use similar information to estimate the demand for individual authors or book types, such as books on the Civil War.

In estimating the demand for books, the factors considered are limited to a number of different prices charged for a good, different quantities of the good purchased, and different levels of the other important factors. This information is used to estimate a piece of the demand curve that shows how the quantity demand changes as the price is increased or decreased over a small range. Observation of the entire demand curve or of all possible shifts in the demand curve would be too difficult and therefore does not occur.

The percentage change in quantity demanded resulting from a percentage change in price is represented by the *price elasticity of demand*, which is the percentage change in quantity demand divided by the percentage change in price. This is shown in equation 2.1.

$$\varepsilon = \frac{\dfrac{Q_1 - Q_2}{(Q_1 + Q_2)/2}100\%}{\dfrac{P_1 - P_2}{(P_1 + P_2)/2}100\%} = \frac{\dfrac{\delta Q}{Q}100\%}{\dfrac{\delta P}{P}100\%} = \frac{\delta QP}{\delta PQ} \qquad (2.1)$$

In this equation, δQ indicates the change in quantity; δP indicates the change in price. The numerator in the first part of equation 2.1 is the percentage change in quantity using the average quantity as a base; i.e., the change in quantity demanded divided by the average quantity multiplied by 100 percent. The denominator is the change in price divided by the average price multiplied by 100 percent.

Sometimes the price elasticity of demand is shown as a negative number because as the price increases (a positive change) quantity demanded decreases (a negative change). In this text, the absolute value of the price elasticity will be used and the price elasticity will always be represented as a positive number.

A price elasticity of 3.59 means that a 1 percent increase in price will result in a 3.59 percent decrease in quantity demanded. A price elasticity of 0.5 means that a 10 percent decrease in price will result in a 5 percent increase in quantity demanded. Using the prices and quantities shown in table 2.1, the price elasticity of demand for Civil War books, calculated from the mid-point of each price range, is shown in table 2.2.

Table 2.2.
The Price Elasticity of Demand for Civil War Books.

Price	Percentage Change	Quantity	Percentage Change	Price Elasticity
$50		11,000		
$45	10.54%	13,000	16.67%	1.58
$40	11.76%	15,000	14.29%	1.22
$35	13.33%	17,000	12.50%	0.94
$30	15.39%	19,000	11.11%	0.72

If the average price of a book on the Civil War were somewhere between $45 and $50, a 10 percent decrease in the price would result in an approximately 1.58 percent increase in the number of Civil War books sold. If the hypothetical numbers in table 2.1 and table 2.2 were accurate, publishers of books on the Civil War could use these price elasticities to determine how sales will change as the market price changes.

In addition to these market price elasticities, individual publishers can calculate the price elasticity for the books they sell. The price elasticity for books on the Civil War by a single publisher will be higher than the price elasticity for the entire market. For example, given the price elasticities in table 2.2, an individual publisher will find the price elasticity at prices between $35 and $40 to be significantly greater than 0.94. This is because consumers have near-perfect substitutes for books from any individual publisher. If any one publisher tries to increase prices unilaterally, consumers are likely to purchase books from other publishers who sell similar titles. Therefore, the percentage change in quantity sold as a result of a price increase will be greater for any individual publisher than for the market as a whole.

The price elasticity of demand is *elastic* if the price elasticity is greater than one. The price elasticity of demand is *inelastic* if the price elasticity is less than one. Using the previous example, the price elasticity at any price between $30 and $40 is inelastic, while the price elasticity in this range for an individual publisher is likely to be elastic.

Elastic and inelastic demand curves are illustrated in figure 2.5 and figure 2.6. Figure 2.5 shows a perfectly elastic demand curve where a slight decrease in price results in an infinite percentage increase in quantity sold. A producer in a market with many other competing producers may face a perfectly elastic demand curve for his product. Any slight increase in the price will result in a significant decrease in sales. Examples may include the demand for a single producer's inexpensive radio or the demand for use of a single photo-copy machine among a set of 10 at the library. If the price per copy at a single photocopy machine were one cent less than the other photocopiers, individuals would be continuously using the less expensive machine while the other nine were idle.

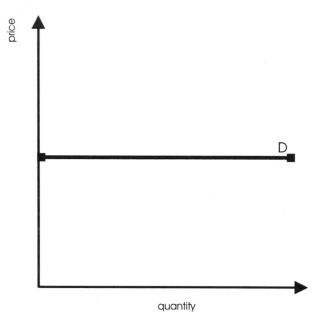

Figure 2.5. Elastic Demand Curve.

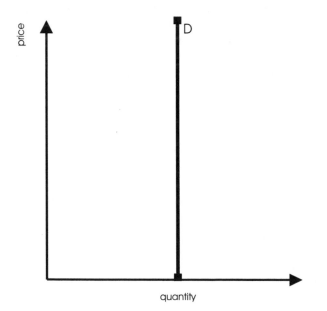

Figure 2.6. Inelastic Demand Curve.

Figure 2.6 shows a perfectly inelastic demand curve where a significant change in price results in no change in the quantity sold. A good or service that is extremely valuable, important, or necessary may have an inelastic demand curve, in which case an increase in the price will not result in consumers decreasing their purchases. Examples of goods with an inelastic demand curve may include core academic journals at a university library or medical information in a hospital emergency room.

Bebensee, Strauch, and Strauch (1989) demonstrated that an inelastic demand for journal subscriptions by academic libraries was an important factor in the price increases by publishers of academic journals.[3] Likewise, Woolsey and Strauch (1992), and Chressanthis and Chressanthis (1994) showed how an inelastic journal demand enables foreign publishers to pass on much of the exchange rate risk to libraries in the United States.[4]

The price elasticity of demand also demonstrates how total revenues (price times quantity) change as the price changes. If the price elasticity is elastic, then an increase in price will decrease revenue while a decrease in price will increase revenue. When the price elasticity is inelastic, an increase in price will increase revenues while a decrease in price will decrease revenues. Therefore, if the price elasticity is 3.4, a 1 percent increase in price will result in a 3.4 percent decrease in quantity sold. Because the quantity sold decreases by a greater percentage than the price increases, total revenues will decrease. However, if the price elasticity is 0.5, then a 10 percent increase in the price will decrease quantity by only 5 percent. In this case, total revenues will increase.

Several economists have estimated the price elasticity of the market demand for different information goods and services. Table 2.3 shows some of these estimates.

Kingma's (1994) estimate of 0.62 implies that a 10 percent increase in the price of photocopying at academic libraries will decrease the number of photocopies by 6.2 percent. If the average price of a photocopy is $0.10 and the average number of photocopies in a year at a given academic library is 1,000,000, then an increase in the price to $0.11 will decrease the total number of photocopies by 62,000 to 938,000. Total revenues from photocopying will increase from $100,000 to $103,180. Three of the four papers cited in table 2.3 show price elasticities less than one, indicating that a price increase will increase total revenues. On the other hand, Crandall (1990) shows a price elasticity greater than one, implying that consumers react strongly to an increase in the price of basic cable service. A 10 percent increase in the price of basic cable will decrease the quantity demanded by 22 percent and decrease total revenue.

Table 2.3.
Estimates of the Price Elasticity of Demand.[5]

Author(s)	Good or Service	Price Elasticity of Demand	Notes
Daly, G., and Mayor, T.	Telephone calls to directory assistance	0.15	Data from communities where directory assistance is priced at $0.10 versus $0.20
Lankford, H.	Elementary and secondary education	0.62	Data from school referendums on public education in Marshall, Michigan
Crandall, R.	Basic cable service	2.20	Average elasticity, data from TCI-owned and -operated systems
Kingma, B.	Photocopying in academic libraries	0.62	Survey data from academic libraries

Consumer Welfare

The demand for a good is used not only to determine how much of a good will be purchased at a given price but is also used to quantify the value or benefit a consumer derives from his or her purchase. This benefit is called *consumer welfare*, and it can be quantified by looking at the consumer's total benefits, marginal benefits, net benefits, and consumer surpluses.

The amount a consumer is willing to pay for a good is a measure of the benefit the consumer receives from it. For example, according to table 2.1, if the cost of a book is $50, Patrick is willing to buy one book, no more, no less. If Patrick's benefit for the book were less than $50, he would not be willing to pay that much. On the other hand, if Patrick's benefit from that book was more than $50, he would be willing to buy more books at that price. If Patrick's benefit from the first book were more than $50, he might purchase one more book every five years (or another 0.2 books per year). Therefore, Patrick's benefit can be defined as the amount he is willing to pay for a book. Patrick's demand curve for books on the Civil War can be used to calculate the number of books he would be willing to purchase at a given price.

Patrick's *marginal benefit* from a purchase is the additional benefit he receives from purchasing one more book, as defined by his willingness to pay for an additional book. If the price of a book is $50, the price for purchasing one more book is $50, and the marginal benefit for purchasing that first book is $50. If the purchase price of a book is $45, the price for purchasing one more book is $45, and the marginal benefit is $45. Patrick's marginal benefits from the first, second, third, and fourth books are represented by the shaded areas on figure 2.7, which were calculated according to the equation (price x number of books) - [price x (number of books - 1)]. This equation yields a rectangle one book wide and as tall as the price on the demand curve (see fig. 2.7).

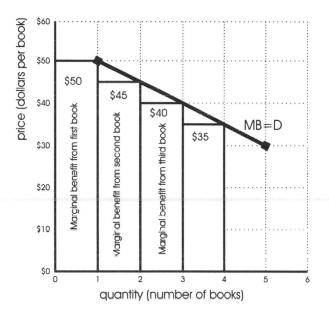

Figure 2.7. Patrick's Marginal and Total Benefit from Books.

Patrick's *total benefit* from a given number of books is calculated by figuring the sum of the marginal benefits from each book purchased. Patrick's total benefit from one book is $50, from two books is $95 ($50 + $45), from three books is $135 ($50 + $45 + $40), etc.

Amount paid is calculated by multiplying the price per book by the number of books. Therefore, according to figure 2.7, the amount paid for the three books purchased at a price of $40 per book is $120. *Consumer surplus* is calculated by subtracting the amount paid from the total benefit. If the total benefit from three books is $135 and Patrick pays $40 per book, the consumer surplus is $15.

As with Patrick's individual purchases, in the entire market for books on the Civil War each book sold has a marginal benefit, total benefit, amount paid, and consumer surplus. This is shown in figure 2.8. The marginal benefit is the area of a small rectangle for each book. The total benefit is the sum of the small rectangles. This area can be approximated by calculating the area under the demand curve in figure 2.8. The amount paid is simply the quantity purchased times the purchase price. For 15,000 books purchased at a price of $40 per book, the amount paid is $600,000. The consumer surplus of the market for books on the Civil War is the difference between the total benefit and the amount paid. This can be approximated by the area of the top triangle in figure 2.8.

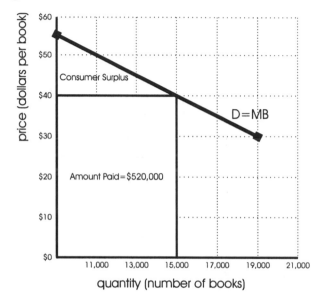

Figure 2.8. Consumer Surplus from Books.

The amount of consumer surplus changes as the price of the good changes. As demonstrated in figure 2.9, as the price of a Civil War book decreases from $40 to $35, the quantity purchased increases, the total benefit from Civil War books increases, the amount paid changes from $600,000 (15,000 copies at $40) to $595,000 (17,000 copies at $35), and the consumer surplus increases. The increase in consumer surplus comes from the consumer savings derived from a lower price paid on the initial purchases of Civil War books plus the net benefits consumers derive from additional purchases of 15,000 to 17,000 books.

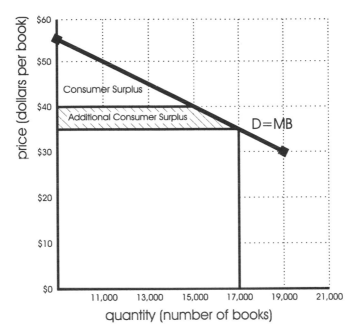

Figure 2.9. Market Consumer Surplus from Books as Price Decreases.

Every good and service has a marginal benefit, a total benefit, and consumer surplus. Further examples of consumer surplus can be found in Lewis (1989), and Kingma and Eppard (1992), who illustrate the consumer surplus of academic journals; Kingma, who measures the consumer surplus from photocopying (1994); and Daly and Mayor (1980), who measure the consumer surplus from directory assistance.[6]

Summary

Consumer theory includes a number of economic tools that enable definition and measurement of the influence of price, income, prices of related goods, and changes in consumer tastes on the demand for goods and services. The price elasticity of demand measures the impact of price on quantity demanded of a good or service, showing the responsiveness of consumers to changes in the price of a product.

Consumer theory also includes tools to measure the value of goods and services to consumers. Marginal benefit, total benefit, and consumer surplus are all useful ways to quantify the value to individuals of their consumption of goods and services. When combined with the cost of producing these goods or services, the tools of welfare economics allow judgments to be made about how much of a particular good should be produced, what types of services should be offered, and which consumers derive the most welfare or surplus from their purchases. Consumer surplus enables measurement of the benefits of managerial and policy decisions.

Discussion Questions

1. Explain how elastic or inelastic the goods in the following sets are relative to each other: 1) hours of watching television, hours of watching a single television station, and hours of watching public television; 2) medical information on headaches and medical information on cancer; and 3) movies, videos, and a video of a particular movie.

2. Consider the demand curve for a popular word-processing software. How does a change in the price of a software program influence the demand for this software? How does a change in the price of personal computers influence the demand for word-processing software?

3. "Information on how to prevent the spread of HIV is free, there is no price charged; therefore, there must be little consumer surplus generated by this information." Comment: Does the price charged for a product always reflect the amount of consumer surplus generated from it?

Notes

1. Bruce R. Kingma, "An Accurate Measurement of the Crowd-Out Effect, Income Effect, and Price Effect for Charitable Contributions," *Journal of Political Economy* (1989): 1197-1207.

2. Jean Walstrom Haley and James Talaga, "Academic Library Responses to Journal Price Discrimination," *College & Research Libraries* (1992): 61-70.

3. Mark Bebensee, Bruce Strauch, and Katina Strauch, "Elasticity and Journal Pricing," *The Acquisitions Librarian* (1989): 219-28.

4. W. William Woolsey and A. Bruce Strauch, "The Impact of U.S. Dollar Depreciation on the Prices of Foreign Academic Journals: A Supply and Demand Analysis," *Publishing Research Quarterly* (1992): 74-81; and George A. Chressanthis and June D. Chressanthis, "A General Econometric Model of the Determinants of Library Subscription Prices and Scholarly Journals: The Role of Exchange Rate Risk and Other Factors," *The Library Quarterly* 64 (1994): 270-93.

5. R. W. Crandall, "Elasticity of Demand for Cable Service and the Effect of Broadcast Signals on Cable Prices," (Appended to TCI Reply Comments in FCC Mass Media Docket, 1990): 90-4; George Daly and Thomas Mayor, "Estimating the Value of a Missing Market: The Economics of Directory Assistance," *Journal of Law and Economics* (1980): 147-66; Bruce R. Kingma, "The Demand for Photocopies and Journal Subscriptions: An Empirical Test of the Librarians' Solution to Journal Pricing" (unpublished manuscript, School of Information Science and Policy, University at Albany, 1994); Hamilton Lankford, "Preferences of Citizens for Public Expenditures on Elementary and Secondary Education," *Journal of Econometrics* (1985): 1-20.

6. David W. Lewis, "Economics of the Scholarly Journal," *College & Research Libraries* (1989): 674-88; Bruce R. Kingma and Philip B. Eppard, "Journal Price Escalation and the Market for Information: The Librarians' Solution," *College & Research Libraries* (1992): 523-35; Bruce R. Kingma, "The Demand for Photocopies and Journal Subscriptions: An Empirical Test of the Librarians' Solution to Journal Pricing" (1994); and George Daly and Thomas Mayor, "Estimating the Value of a Missing Market: The Economics of Directory Assistance" (1980): 147-66.

The Cost of Output and Market Supply

3

To produce output, either in goods or services, an organization must purchase and combine inputs. The cost of producing a unit of output is the cost of the inputs necessary to make it. Nonprofit organizations, for-profit organizations, libraries, and government agencies must employ labor, land, buildings, computers, paper, and other resources to provide legal services, books, computer software, reference services, or other goods or services.

The goals of a firm determine how managers in that organization decide on its level of output, given the costs and productivity of inputs and the profitability, social value, or other perceived benefit of outputs. A for-profit firm produces output to make profit; its goal is to maximize profit. Nonprofit firms and government organizations typically produce a good or service, maximizing the social value of that output; they are not trying to gain profit from the output. A government agency may produce outputs to maximize social welfare, government employment, the welfare of some constituency, or the budget of the agency. In each case, it is important to quantify the costs of producing the good or service.

Fixed and Variable Costs

The cost of an output can be divided into two types: fixed costs and variable costs. *Fixed costs* are costs that do not change as the level of output increases within a specified period of time. Regardless of the level of production, within the time period given, fixed costs, some-times referred to as set-up costs, overhead, or first-copy costs in publishing, cannot be changed. For example, the cost of the factory or a library building is a fixed cost within a year. No matter what the level of output that goes on during a year in that building, the cost will be the same. The cost of the author's time is a fixed cost for the printing of a particular book within one month. Similarly, the cost of the mainframe computer is a fixed cost for the production of university computer resources over the next month. In each case these costs are necessary to produce even the first unit of output and cannot be changed within the time period specified.

Variable costs are costs that increase as the level of output increases within a given period of time. The cost of employees for a car factory or a library, the cost of paper for copies, the cost of books purchased, or the cost of paper and printing are all examples of variable costs. In each case, the variable input must be increased to increase the units of output. To increase library services, employee hours must be increased. To increase the number of copies made with a photocopier, the amount of paper and toner must be increased. To increase the number of copies of a particular book the amount of paper, labor, and printing must be increased.

Fixed and variable costs are defined by the output and the period of time chosen. If the goal is to increase production over the next month, the variable costs are those that can realistically be changed within that time period. Over a longer period of time, more costs are variable. Skilled labor is frequently a fixed cost in a month, but given a longer period of time, it can become a variable cost. It may take several months to train librarians in a corporate library to the level at which they can be considered fully productive. In a month, the salaries of corporate librarians may be a fixed cost in the production of library services. However, given a year, more librarians can be hired and trained; therefore, their salaries are variable costs given the longer time period.

For any particular good or service, there is usually a "common sense" division of fixed and variable costs and period of time for production. Inputs fixed for one good are more naturally defined as variable for another. For example, the author's time and first-copy costs in publishing a book are fixed costs, which must be incurred regardless of the number of copies that will be printed and sold. The printing of individual copies of the book is a variable cost. This provides a logical split of fixed and variable costs if production of a book title over the next one to three months were to be examined.

However, over a time period much greater that one to three months (for example, an entire year), the authors' time and set-up costs become variable costs. Over a year, a publisher can hire other authors to write additional book titles, employ more labor, and purchase additional paper to print copies of the publisher's collection of titles. Over a year, publishers make decisions about not only how many copies of individual titles to produce but also how many authors to employ. However, it would still be difficult for a publisher to build and occupy a new building in a year, so the building may still reasonably be classified as a fixed cost.

Table 3.1.
Fixed and Variable Costs of Production.

Goods and Services	Time Period	Fixed Costs	Variable Costs
Copies of a novel	One month	Editing, typesetting, author's time and effort, the building	Ink, paper, labor, and postage for copies of the novel; marketing costs
Book publishing	One year	The building	Cost per copy, authors' time, set-up costs
Copies of a software program	Three months	Time and effort of programmers	Packaging, floppy disks, and labor for copies
Books from the library	One year	The library building	Librarians and books
Photocopies	One day	Purchase of the photocopy machine	Paper, toner for individual copy
Minutes of telephone service	One day	Telephone, circuits, and network	An electric current, sometimes an operator
Viewing a television broadcast	One hour	Labor, building, cameras, script, video, electricity	The electricity to power a television set (provided by the consumer)
Television broadcasting	One year	Television building and broadcast equipment	Labor, cameras, scripts, electricity

Table 3.1 gives several examples of fixed and variable costs for information goods and services. In each case, fixed inputs and variable inputs must be combined to produce units of the given output. While fixed inputs must be employed to start production, variable inputs must be purchased to increase the production of the output within the time period. For longer periods of time, more costs are variable.

Marginal, Average, and Total Costs

The *marginal cost* of a unit of output is the cost of increasing output within a given period of time. Marginal costs are the costs of the variable inputs which must be employed to increase output. For example, the marginal cost of an additional copy of a software program is about $0.50, the cost of a floppy disk. The marginal cost of an additional hour of reference services at the library is the hourly wage of a reference librarian. The marginal cost of copies of a particular book title is the cost of printing one more copy of the book.

If calculated over a year, this publisher has the time to hire additional authors and produce additional titles as well as additional copies of existing titles. Therefore, the costs of the authors' time and the set-up costs for titles produced within the year are included as marginal costs.

The *average cost* of a unit of output is the per unit cost of output, the total cost divided by the total output over a given period of time. Average costs include the cost of fixed inputs or overhead, figures that are usually left out of marginal costs.

Average costs define the price per unit of output necessary for the firm to break even, in other words, the price at which the unit should be sold such that revenues equal costs. If a good costs, on average, $50 per unit, and the units are sold at a price of $50 each, then the seller breaks even. If the price of a unit of output exceeds the average cost per unit then the firm will make a profit. If the price is less than the average cost, then the firm will operate at a loss.

Total cost is the sum of the marginal costs. Table 3.2 illustrates the total, average, and marginal costs and profit for a hypothetical publisher of books on the Civil War in a given year. For example, at an output level of 2,100 books, the marginal cost per book, the cost to make the next book, is $31. The total cost for books at the next level, 2,200, is the sum of the marginal costs. To calculate this, take the previous total cost ($72,600 at an output of 2,100) and add the marginal costs for increasing output by 100 books ($32 x 100 = $3,200) to get a new total cost of $75,800. The average price of a book is the total cost divided by the output, or at an output of 2,200, $75,800 ÷ 2,200 = $34.45.

For more discussion of the concepts of marginal, average, and total costs, refer to appendix A (p. 171).

Table 3.2 demonstrates a standard assumption in economics: that the marginal cost increases as the output (number of books) increases. This is because as more books are produced, there is more wear and tear on the publishing equipment, and more labor is required. In addition, as more titles are produced, the publisher has a more difficult time finding competent authors to write books on the Civil War. As more labor, paper, authors, and other variable factors are employed, they must all use the same fixed factors (e.g., the building and equipment). But as more variable inputs are employed, they begin to crowd and congest the fixed factor. As a result, while at first, increasing the output by increasing variable inputs lowers the average cost per unit of output, once the fixed factors have reached the peak level of efficiency, each additional unit of the variable input is slightly less productive, increasing the cost per unit of the output. Table 3.2 illustrates this point. The lowest average cost per book ($34.38) occurs when output is at 2,400 units and the marginal cost per book is $34. After that, the average cost per book begins to rise as marginal costs per book increase.

Table 3.2.
The Costs of Publishing.

Output	Total Cost	Average Cost per Book	Marginal Cost per Book	Profit (Price = $40)
2,000	$69,500	$34.75		$10,500
2,100	$72,600	$34.57	$31	$11,400
2,200	$75,800	$34.45	$32	$12,200
2,300	$79,100	$34.39	$33	$12,900
2,400	$82,500	$34.38	$34	$13,500
2,500	$86,000	$34.40	$35	$14,000
2,600	$89,600	$34.46	$36	$14,400
2,700	$93,300	$34.56	$37	$14,700
2,800	$97,100	$34.68	$38	$14,900
2,900	$101,000	$34.83	$39	$15,000
3,000	$105,000	$35.00	$40	$15,000
3,100	$109,100	$35.19	$41	$14,900
3,200	$113,300	$35.41	$42	$14,700
3,300	$117,600	$35.64	$43	$14,400
3,400	$122,000	$35.88	$44	$14,000
3,500	$126,500	$36.14	$45	$13,500

This diminishing productivity of the variable factor is a result of the fixed factor, which is constrained by the limited time period, one year, for production. Within one year, as the publisher tries to produce more books on the Civil War, it becomes impossible to increase the level of fixed factors to increase production. The publisher is constrained by the size of his building and speed of his publishing equipment. Additionally, within a limited period of time, increasing output by employing more variable input congests the fixed input (i.e., you can only ask employees to work a certain number of hours before you have to pay them overtime, which increases costs, or they start to get tired, which decreases productivity).

At first, the notion of increasing marginal costs of production seems counter-intuitive. If a unit of output can be produced at some given cost per unit, then it would seem that additional units of output can be produced at the same or perhaps a lower cost per unit. However, the notion that output can be increased at a lower unit cost frequently confuses the increase in production in the short run, within a limited time period, and production in the long run, when fixed and variable inputs are adjustable. In other words, given a longer period of time, the level of fixed factors can be increased. In this case, the publisher can rent or build a larger building or more office space.

As the scale of production is increased, frequently the firm experiences *economies of scale*. Economies of scale occur when the average cost of output decreases as output is increased when fixed and variable factors are adjustable. For example, assume a publisher produces 10,000 books per year on the Civil War but can double output to 20,000 by doubling the number of employees and the size of his firm, but not hiring additional management. In this case, managerial costs remain the same, and the average cost per unit will decrease as the level of overhead is shared among additional units of output. If the original 10,000 books per year were produced at an average cost of $30 per book, increasing output to 20,000 units may lower the average costs to $25 per book.

Diseconomies of scale occur when average costs increase as output is increased when fixed and variable factors are adjustable. Such diseconomies of scale may occur when additional layers of management are employed by growing firms. In this case, a doubling of output may occur, but only when costs more than double, resulting in an increase in the average cost per year.

Several studies have estimated the cost structure of information markets. Baumol and Braunstein (1977) found evidence of economies of scale over some ranges of output for journal publishing in the 1970s.[1] Chressanthis (1995) tested for the cost structure of academic libraries and the influence of changes in circulation, interlibrary loan, reference transactions, and total volumes on costs.[2] The cost structure of public libraries, universities, book publishing, advertising, cable television, the music recording industry, telecommunications, and other industries has also been studied.[3]

Supply

While table 3.2 shows the cost of publishing books on the Civil War, it does not indicate what level of production the publisher will choose. The number of Civil War books a publisher is willing to produce depends on the market price he believes he can get for those books. In part, this depends on how competitive the publisher believes the market for Civil

War books is. In this chapter, the assumption will be made that the publisher is one of five publishers of Civil War books, a very competitive market. Each publisher would like to undercut the price of the competing publishers, if possible, to increase market share, and any individual publisher may assume that she cannot significantly increase the price of her book without losing a significant number of customers to other publishers. If one publisher sells books on the Civil War for $50 and all other publishers sell books of comparable quality for $40, most consumers will purchase the $40 books. Therefore, it can be assumed that each publisher is a "price-taker" who accepts the going market price as the price she can charge for a Civil War book.

The Supply Curve

A publisher will sell Civil War books as long as he makes a profit on them. The number of books the publisher will offer on the market is determined by weighing the marginal costs with the marginal benefits, the value expected for a good or service. If the current market price of a book is $40, the publisher expects to receive a marginal benefit of $40 per book. Therefore, a producer will make and sell a good until the marginal cost just equals the market price. The publisher represented in table 3.2 will offer 3,000 books for sale. If he offers only 2,800 books, he will lose the benefit of the 200 additional books that have a marginal cost less than $40. The 2,900th book has a marginal cost of $39. If the publisher sells that book at $40, he would make $1 per book in profit. However, if the publisher produces 3,100 books, the marginal cost of each book is greater than the purchase price of $40. The marginal cost of the 3,100th book is $41 and would decrease profits by $1 per book if sold at the going market price of $40. Based on table 3.2, if the current market price of a book is $45, this publisher will supply 3,500 books to the market, and if the market price is $35, the publisher will supply 2,500 books. As the price publishers believe they can sell a book for increases, the number of books they are willing to supply to the market increases, based on the marginal cost per book.

Figure 3.1 illustrates the marginal costs (MC), average costs (AC), and profit for the hypothetical publishing firm from table 3.2. The marginal cost curve shows the quantity of books that the firm is willing to supply to the market at each price. As on table 3.2, average costs curves are U-shaped, initially decreasing and then increasing. *Total revenue* is the quantity multiplied by the price (PQ) or area (0,Q,E,P) in figure 3.1. *Total cost* is the quantity multiplied by the average cost of each unit at that level of output, Q(AC), or area (0,Q,F,AC) in figure 3.1. *Profit* is the difference between total revenue (PQ) and total costs Q(AC), or the shaded area (PQ-Q(AC)) on figure 3.1.

Figure 3.2 illustrates a *market supply curve,* which is the total sum of units supplied to the market by all the publishers at a given price. In our hypothetical market for Civil War books, if the market price is $40, each of the five publishers will offer 3,000 books for a total of 15,000 books. At a price of $45, each publisher would supply 3,500 books for a total of 17,500 books.

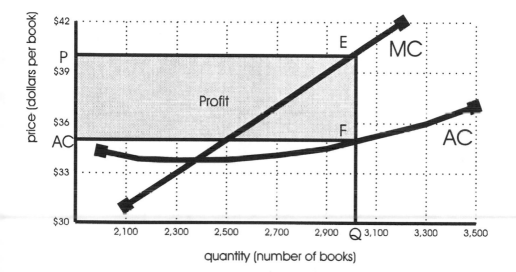

Figure 3.1. Producer Costs and Profit.

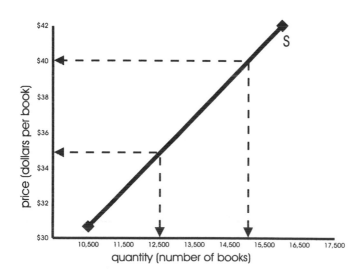

Figure 3.2. Market Supply Curve.

Input Costs and Changes in Technology

In addition to the market price, the cost of inputs and current technology influence the market supply of a good or service. If the cost of inputs (e.g., the cost of ink, paper, wages, etc.) increases, publisher costs for all units of output will increase. In this case, publishers will not be willing to produce the last few, high-cost units of output for sale at the current market price. This change in the market supply is illustrated in figure 3.3 as a shift from S to S'. At each price level, supply curve S' demonstrates that publishers are not willing to produce as many books when the costs of inputs are higher. If the price of inputs were to fall, then the supply curve would shift from S' back to S.

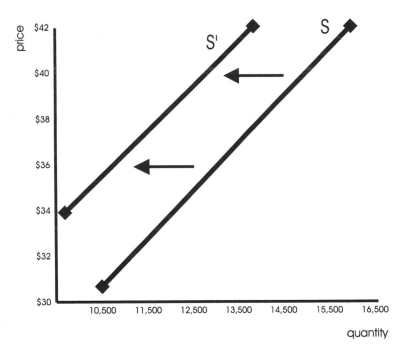

Figure 3.3. Shift in Market Supply After an Increase in Cost of Input.

In the same way, when technology changes market supply also changes. For example, if a new method of printing were developed that required less labor and materials for each book, the supply of books would increase at every price. If S' were the original supply curve, a change in technology that lowered the cost of production would be represented by a shift in the supply curve from S' to S.

The Price Elasticity of Supply

The slope of a supply or cost curve indicates how responsive output is to changes in price and, frequently, how marginal costs change as output changes. The price elasticity of supply measures the responsiveness of supply to changes in the market price. The price elasticity of supply is defined as the percentage change in quantity supplied resulting from a 1 percent change in price. Formally, this equals

$$\eta = \frac{\dfrac{\delta Q}{Q} 100\%}{\dfrac{\delta P}{P} 100\%} = \frac{\delta Q}{\delta P} \frac{P}{Q} \tag{3.1}$$

where δQ is the change in quantity supplied and δP is the change in the market price. The price elasticity of supply is a number somewhere between zero and infinity. When the price elasticity of supply is greater than 1, supply is *elastic*, meaning that if the market price increases, producers can increase the market supply by an even greater percentage. For example, a price elasticity of supply of 1.2 means that a 10% increase in the market price would induce producers to increase supply by 12%. When the price elasticity of supply is less than 1, supply is inelastic, in which case there is a limit to the supply that can be made available on the market, regardless of price.

In markets where the marginal cost of production is constant and the market has more than one competitive producer, and if producers could increase supply with little increase in the price, supply would be perfectly elastic and the price elasticity of supply would equal infinity. In this case, even a slight increase in the market price results in producers being able and willing to sell more of a particular good or service.

For example, consider the supply of pencils. There are many companies, both national and local, that make pencils and sell them at a price of about $0.10 per pencil. If any one producer were to price their pencils at $0.20 per pencil, they would lose business to their competitors. This makes pencil producers price-takers; in other words, each accepts the going market price of $0.10 per pencil. Yet each firm is capable of producing a considerable number of pencils as long as sales remain high enough at this price to generate a profit. Given this, one might safely assume that the supply of pencils might be perfectly elastic and might look something like figure 3.4.

Conversely, in some markets the price elasticity of supply is perfectly inelastic, equal to zero. For example, the supply of new novels by Charles Dickens can be used for consideration. While it is possible to reproduce existing Dickens novels, it is impossible to produce a new Dickens novel because Mr. Dickens is no longer producing novels; he is dead. Therefore, regardless of the price of a new Dickens novel, there exist a fixed number of them. Figure 3.5 illustrates the inelastic supply of Dickens novels.

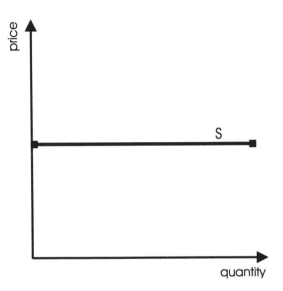

Figure 3.4. Perfectly Elastic Supply Curve.

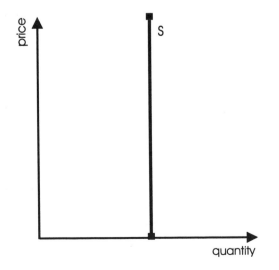

Figure 3.5. Perfectly Inelastic Supply Curve.

Summary

The costs of production of a good or service can be divided into fixed and variable costs, depending on the period of time over which calculations are made. These concepts of cost can be used to define *marginal cost*—the cost per additional unit—and *average cost*—the cost per unit. Increasing marginal costs results in producers increasing supply as the price increases. This effect on the quantity of product supplied to the market based on the market price is defined as the price elasticity of supply. As shall be seen in the next chapter, supply and demand are combined in a market to determine the quantity sold and the price charged in the market.

Increasing marginal costs is a standard assumption for most markets; however, in subsequent chapters it will be demonstrated that this assumption does not hold for many information goods and services, which can frequently be reproduced at low marginal costs. Many information goods have fixed costs far more significant than the variable costs of reproduction. As a result, the standard market analysis described in the next chapter must be modified under certain circumstances.

Discussion Questions

1. Fixed and variables costs for goods and services depend on how these services are defined. Consider the fixed and variable costs for servicing the following: a) library patrons; b) library patrons who ask reference questions; c) library patrons who check out books; and d) library patrons who do not return their books on time. How is the cost for each type of service different? Why is it important to consider these differences?

2. Consider the average and marginal cost curves shown in figures 3.6, 3.7, and 3.8. Discuss the differences between these cost curves. What do these figures tell you about the production of these goods?

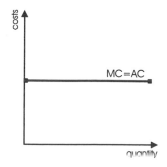

Figure 3.6.

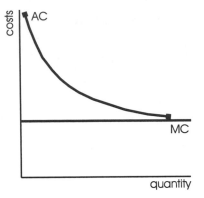

Figure 3.7.

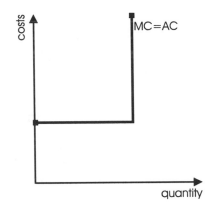

Figure 3.8.

3. Choose some library service (i.e., reference, circulation, cataloging, technical services, etc.), describe the fixed and variable costs of that service, and write what you think these costs might be. Calculate the total, average, and marginal cost of that service in a table similar to table 3.2.

Notes

1. William J. Baumol and Yale M. Braunstein, "Empirical Study of Scale Economies and Production Complementarity: The Case of Journal Publication," *The Journal of Political Economy* 85, no. 5 (1977): 1037-48.

2. George A. Chressanthis, "The Cost Structure and Benefit Impact of Academic Libraries at American Research Universities," in *Economics of Information: Conference Proceedings* (Lyon, France, ENSSIB, 1995).

3. See Larry DeBoer, "Economies of Scale and Input Substitution in Public Libraries," *Journal of Urban Economics* 32, no. 2 (September 1992): 257-68; Hans de Groot, Walter McMahon, and Fredericks J. Volkwein, "The Cost Structure of American Research Universities," *Review of Economics and Statistics* 73, no. 3 (1991): 424-31; George Bittlingmayer, "The Elasticity of Demand for Books, Resale Price Maintenance and the Lerner Index," *Journal of Institutional and Theoretical Economics* 148, no. 4 (1992): 588-606; Alvin J. Silk and Ernst R. Berndt, "Scale and Scope Effects on Advertising Agency Costs," *Marketing Science* 12, no. 1 (1993): 53-72; Robert N. Rubinovitz, "Market Power and Price Increases for Basic Cable Service Since Deregulation," *Rand Journal of Economics* 24, no. 1 (1993): 1-18; Peter J. Alexander, "Entry Barriers, Release Behavior, and Multi-Product Firms in the Music Recording Industry," *Review of Industrial Organization* 9, no. 1 (1994): 85-98; and Francis J. Cronin, et al., "Telecommunications and Cost Savings in Health Care Services," *Southern Economic Journal* 61, no. 2 (1994): 343-55.

Market Equilibrium and Economic Efficiency

In 1776, Adam Smith in *The Wealth of Nations* described the market as a place where consumers and producers come together to buy and sell and auction and bargain, changing prices and output until an equilibrium market price and market level of output is determined.[1] The "law of the invisible hand" says that within a market consumers and producers bargain over the price of a good, ultimately settling on an equilibrium price. If the price is too high, producers will be left with a surplus and be forced to lower their price. If the price is too low, shortages will result and consumers will be willing to pay more for the limited supply, ultimately bidding up the price. In the end, goes the theory, the 'invisible hand' pushes the market to an equilibrium price that consumers are willing to pay and producers are willing to accept as payment. Today's market price of a daily newspaper is $0.50; the market price for renting a movie on video is $3; and the market price for a new book on the Civil War is about $40. In each case, consumers voluntarily exchange cash to sellers for a good or service.

Economics is the study of the allocation of scarce goods, and prices are a mechanism for the allocation of those goods. Prices determine who purchases a good or service. Consumers who are willing to pay the price for a good receive it, while those who cannot pay that price do not. Prices also determine who produces a good or service. Producers are entrepreneurs and managers who feel that they can make a profit by selling a particular good at a given price. Producers who cannot sell the good at a price consumers are willing to pay cannot make a profit and ultimately go out of business. The resulting market price and level of sales is the market equilibrium, separating consumers who are willing to pay for a good from those who cannot and separating producers who can efficiently produce the good from those who cannot.

Market Equilibrium

The *market equilibrium* is a price and quantity such that consumers are willing to purchase the amount producers are willing to supply at a particular price. The market combines consumer demand with producer supply of a good. The demand for a good or service, described in chapter 2, is the quantity consumers are willing to purchase at a given price. The supply of a good, described in chapter 3, is the quantity producers are willing to sell at a given price. Figure 4.1 combines figure 2.2 (demand) and figure 3.2 (supply) to illustrate the market for books on the Civil War.

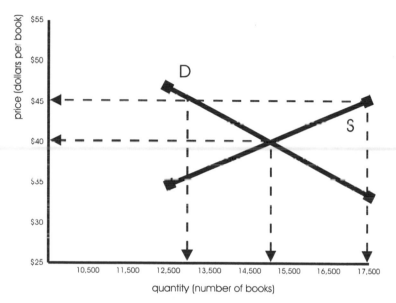

Figure 4.1. Market Equilibrium.

The market equilibrium in figure 4.1 is at a price of $40 and a quantity of 15,000 books.

If a different price and quantity were to prevail, the actions of consumers and producers would return the market to an equilibrium. For example, if the price of books on the Civil War were raised to $45, producers would be willing to supply a total of 17,500 books, according to figure 4.1. At a price of $45, however, consumers are only willing to purchase 13,000 books. The remaining 4,500 books would be left unsold. To sell these surplus books, producers would be forced to lower their prices. As the price falls, consumers will purchase more books. However, at the lower price, producers will not be willing to supply as many books. Ultimately, the two sides of the market will reach equilibrium again at the price of $40 and the quantity of 15,000 books.

Similarly, if the price of Civil War book were reduced to less than $40, consumers would demand more books than producers would be willing to supply at the lower price. For example, if the price were $35, consumers would be willing to purchase 17,000 books, but producers would only be willing to sell 12,500 books, according to figure 4.1. This results in a shortage of books, in which case consumers are willing to pay more for the limited number of books available. This shortage of books results in producers increasing their prices until, once again, the market equilibrium would be reestablished at a price of $40 and a quantity of 15,000 books.

The factors that influence the demand and supply of a good or service will also influence the market equilibrium. For example, if consumer income increases and, as a result, the market demand for books increases, producers will increase the price of their books, and the market equilibrium will move to the new intersection of demand and supply. This is shown in figure 4.2. As demand shifts from D to D', the market equilibrium shifts from $40 and 15,000 books to $45 and 17,500 books.

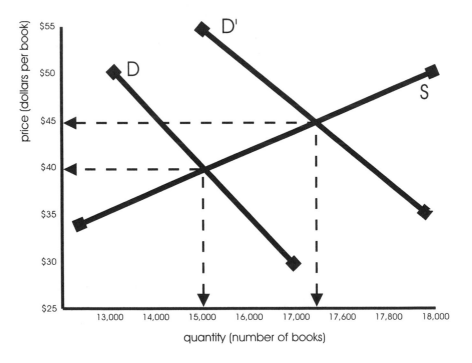

Figure 4.2. Shift in Market Equilibrium Based on Consumer Income Increase.

Changes in the prices of paperback books or other related goods or consumer tastes will also shift the demand for hardcover books on the Civil War and produce a new market equilibrium. A change in the cost of paper or other inputs will shift the supply curve, affecting the market equilibrium.

The Elasticity of Supply and Demand

As the market demand or supply changes, the resulting change in the market equilibrium will be determined by the elasticity of demand and supply. Figure 4.3 shows the effect of an increase in demand in the market for paperback romance novels, a product with an elastic supply curve because additional romance titles and copies of these books can be produced without a significant increase in costs. In this case, an increase in the demand for romance novels will result in an increase in the equilibrium quantity sold but will have little effect on the equilibrium price. Publishers will simply increase the number of books on the shelves to satisfy consumer demand.

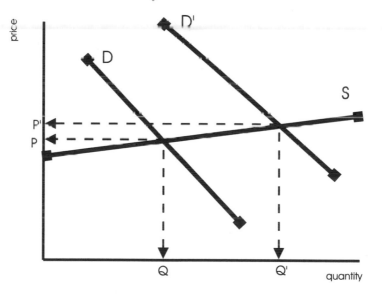

Figure 4.3. Shift in Demand for a Product with an Elastic Supply Curve.

When the demand for a good is elastic, a change in supply will result in a change in the quantity sold, but there will be little change in the price. This is illustrated in figure 4.4. Figure 4.4 illustrates the demand for and supply of romance novels from a particular publisher. Because this is a publisher in a highly competitive market, the demand curve for romance novels by this particular publisher is elastic. In other words, consumers can purchase romance novels from competing publishers and therefore do not have to accept increases in price by any one publisher. As a result, if the costs of production for any single publisher were to increase, that publisher might increase price slightly but is likely to experience a dramatic decline in sales as a result. Figure 4.4 illustrates this effect on the equilibrium price and quantity of books sold by an individual publisher of romance novels. The shift in the supply curve from S to S' produces a slight increase in the price of books by this publisher, P to P', and a dramatic decrease in sales, Q to Q'. An increase in the costs of production for any individual firm in a competitive market or for firms in any market where demand is elastic will have the same result.

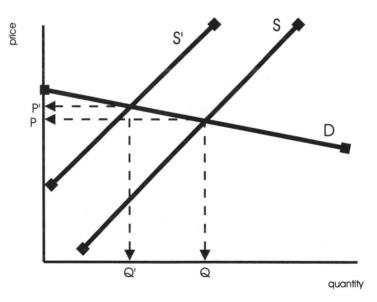

Figure 4.4. Shift in Supply for a Product with an Elastic Demand Curve.

When the demand or supply curve is inelastic, changes in the market produce dramatic changes in price but little change in quantity sold. This is illustrated in figure 4.5, which shows the market for first editions of Mark Twain's novels. An increase in the demand for first editions of novels by Mark Twain cannot change the number available, the supply is inelastic (although it may increase the number of unscrupulous dealers selling forgeries). However, any increase in demand will increase the amount required to purchase a first edition Twain novel at an auction. In figure 4.5 the equilibrium price of a first edition Twain novel increases from P to P'.

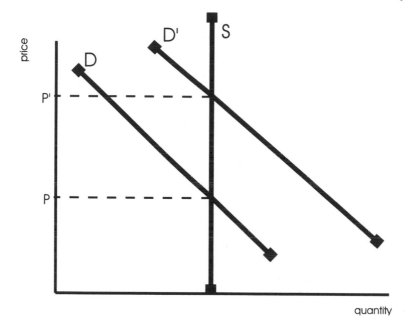

Figure 4.5. Shift in Demand for a Product with an Inelastic Supply Curve.

As figures 4.3, 4.4, and 4.5 illustrate, the more elastic the demand and supply curve, the greater the change in the equilibrium quantity relative to the change in the equilibrium price. If demand and supply are relatively inelastic, the equilibrium price will change by a greater degree than the equilibrium quantity.

Economic Efficiency

Figure 4.1 illustrates the market equilibrium price of Civil War books and, if the consumers and producers are identified, it shows who owns or purchases these books and which publishers printed them. Market forces determine who consumes and produces a particular good, but does this mean that these are the consumers and producers who should receive and provide this good? If an "economically efficient" or "socially efficient" level of production and consumption can be defined, is this the same allocation of goods as that determined in a competitive market? Under what circumstances should the government intervene in a market to increase economic efficiency by offering subsidies or imposing taxes or regulations?

There are many examples of markets upon which the government imposes regulations, subsidies, and taxes and many more markets where someone requests government intervention. Telecommunications law initially established a single provider of telephone service in the United States, then opened the long-distance market to competition. The United States Federal Communications Commission (FCC) regulates radio, telecommunications, and commercial and cable television markets, while copyright, patent, and trade-secret laws regulate what consumers and producers can mimic or copy. The information superhighway, or Internet, was heavily subsidized by the government. In each case, the competitive market equilibrium was altered by the intervention of the government to increase, decrease, or regulate the market.

Competitive market forces determine an equilibrium price, which in turn governs who will purchase the good and who will produce it. However, there are circumstances when it may be in society's best interest to have more or less of a good produced than at the level dictated by market equilibrium. The "socially efficient" level of production may be more or less than the market equilibrium.

How does one determine what is the efficient level of output? Welfare economists usually consider the *pareto optimum* as the *socially efficient* level of output. The pareto optimum is defined as that level of output at which no one person can be made better off without making someone else worse off. Given that those made better off by a change in the market can, theoretically, compensate those made worse off, the pareto optimum, or economically efficient level of output, is the level of production and consumption that maximizes the difference between the benefits from consumption and the costs of production. Therefore, if output is increased and those who benefit from the output receive a greater benefit than the cost, increasing output will increase economic efficiency.

For example, if a vaccine to cure a communicable disease such as AIDS is discovered, it is probably true that the benefit of providing the vaccine to everyone with the disease is greater than the costs of producing it. In this case, it may be necessary for the government to finance the production and distribution of the vaccine. Conversely, if the market produces a level of output such that the costs of producing the good exceed the benefits consumers receive from it, decreasing output will increase economic efficiency. For example, it may soon be that the costs to publishers and the cost to the environment of producing books on paper, which is becoming a scarce resource, may exceed the benefit consumers receive from them. In this case, government regulation or taxation of this market to decrease the level of output might increase economic efficiency. The socially efficient level of output is illustrated in figure 4.6.

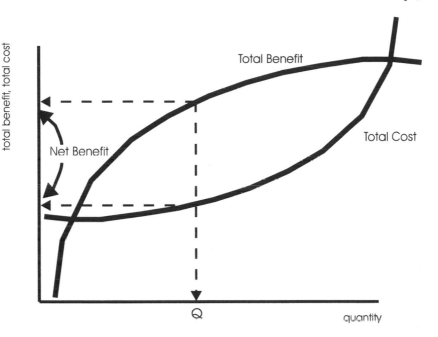

Figure 4.6. Socially Efficient Allocation of Resources.

Figure 4.6 shows the total benefit and total costs from the consumption and production of books. As the number of books purchased increases, the total benefit increases. As the number of books produced increases, the total cost also increases. The difference between the total benefit and total cost is the *net benefit*. Maximum net benefit is achieved at the output level that displays the greatest difference between these two curves. In figure 4.6, maximum benefit is reached at output level Q.

Socially Efficient Competitive Markets

When does a competitive market achieve an economically efficient level of output? When both consumers and producers have full information and there are no benefits or costs external to the market, the competitive market equilibrium is the socially efficient level of output. This is because the consumers with the most benefit from consumption purchase the good, while the producers with the most cost-efficient method of production, sell the good.

The demand-supply diagram developed in chapter 2 and chapter 3 can be used to illustrate the socially efficient level of output. In chapter 2 it was shown how the demand for a good represents the marginal benefit of consumption. In chapter 3 it was shown how the supply of a good, in a competitive market, represents the marginal cost of production. Because the maximum difference between the total benefit and the total cost is the location where the marginal benefit equals the marginal cost, then the competitive market equilibrium is the economically efficient level of output. This is illustrated in figure 4.7.

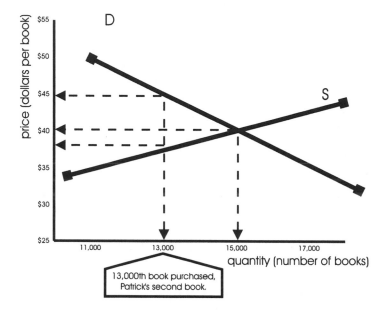

Figure 4.7. When the Competitive Market Achieves Social Efficiency.

Figure 4.7 shows the market equilibrium at the intersection of the demand and supply curves for books on the Civil War. For all books to the left of 15,000 in figure 4.7, the marginal benefit of consumption, as defined by the demand curve (D), is greater than the marginal cost of production, as defined by the supply curve (S). Therefore, each book produced and consumed up to 15,000 increases net economic or social benefit.

Another way to see this is by examining the benefit and costs of each individual book to the left of 15,000. One of the first 13,000 books represents the second book purchased by Patrick from which he received a marginal benefit of $45 (see table 2.1 and figure 2.7). This book can be produced by any one of five publishers at a marginal cost of $36 (see figure 3.1 and table 3.2; each of five publishers produces 2,600 books). The difference between the benefit Patrick receives from this book and the cost to the publisher of producing it is $9. Patrick will benefit from reading this book more than it cost the publisher to make it, so there is a positive net economic benefit from the transaction between Patrick and this publisher of $9. This benefit may end up as a profit to the publisher or as consumer surplus to Patrick. In either case, it provides a benefit to some member of the economy. This positive net benefit from the 13,000th book makes the production and purchase of this book socially efficient.

So to reiterate, for each of the first 15,000 Civil War books produced and consumed, the marginal benefit from that consumption is greater than the marginal cost to society of producing them. However, for books produced and consumed in excess of 15,000, the marginal cost to a publisher of making the book is greater than the marginal benefit a consumer will receive from purchasing it. For example, it is known that one of our consumers, George, receives a marginal benefit of only $35 from purchasing his second book (see table 2.1). This may be the 17,000th book produced. However, the marginal cost of producing this book is $44 (scc tablc 3.2; each of five publishers produces 3,400 books). There is a difference of negative $9 between the benefit George receives from his sccond book and the cost of producing it. In other words, there would be a net economic loss to society of $9 if this book were produced and then purchased by George. If goods are produced at a cost greater than their benefit, social efficiency decreases.

The competitive market equilibrium that results in a price of $40 and a supply of 15,000 books also results in the economically efficient level of production and consumption for society. Consumers who purchase one of the first 15,000 books receive a benefit from their purchase that exceeds the cost of producing the book, while producers who make the first 15,000 books do so at a marginal cost less than the marginal benefit consumers receive. Increasing output beyond the market equilibrium would only decrease economic efficiency as the marginal cost exceeds the marginal benefit of each book after 15,000 books.

In a competitive market the price of the good determines production and consumption. Consumers who receive a benefit greater than the equilibrium price will consume the good, while producers who produce at a cost less than the equilibrium price will supply this good. In the above example, only consumers who receive a marginal benefit greater than $40 will purchase a book, while only publishers with a marginal cost less than $40 will supply books.

In our example, the market equilibrium yields the socially efficient, or pareto optimum level of output. However, this is not true for all goods and services. There are some goods and services for which the competitive market equilibrium fails to achieve the pareto optimum.

Market Failure

When there are costs and benefits in a market that are not represented in the demand and supply curves, or when the market is prevented from reaching the competitive market equilibrium, there is a market failure. A *market failure* occurs when the socially efficient level of output is different from the competitive market equilibrium. An overproduction or underproduction of the good or service may be the result of consumers or producers not taking the external costs or benefits of their actions into account, the lack of a competitive market, or government policies that prevent the market from achieving the socially efficient level of output.

The most obvious and frequently cited example of a market failure is when the production of a good causes pollution. For example, sulfur dioxide and other chemicals are released into the air during the process of making a gallon of paint. This pollution imposes costs on society that are not considered by the producer as part of the firm's costs of production. The manufacturer of paint considers only the costs of labor, capital, and chemicals used in production. Similarly, consumers of paint typically do not consider the pollution caused by the production of paint when they are purchasing it. As a result the market supply and demand for paint does not incorporate the external costs of the pollution produced during the manufacturing process, and there is a market failure.

Pollution is not the only example of market failure, though. Whenever costs or benefits are not fully realized or borne by producers and consumers, there is a possibility that the competitive market equilibrium will differ from the socially efficient level of output. The adverse effects of pollution, false advertising, monopolies, taxes, and other problems may all result in socially inefficient market equilibriums. When a paint factory's production causes pollution or when too many direct mail firms congest mailboxes with advertising, the equilibrium output of paint or junk mail exceeds the pareto optimum, or economically efficient level of output.

Conversely, when all of the benefits of a market are not realized by consumers, when the market is controlled by a single supplier, or when government regulation restricts output, the equilibrium level of output may be less than the pareto optimum. For example, when government taxes or monopolistic firms increase prices above marginal cost, the market will be prevented from reaching the pareto optimum level of output. When consumers do not have full information on the value of a good or service, they may not purchase goods of higher quality simply because they cannot determine which goods are higher quality. As a result, the level of output in the market will be less than the pareto optimum level.

There are four categories of market failure: 1) externalities; 2) public goods; 3) monopolies or monopsonies; and 4) market failure resulting from consumers or producers not having perfect information about the quality of goods or services. Each type of market failure and its application to the economics of information will be discussed in the following chapters.

Summary

The point of intersection of demand and supply curves determines the market equilibrium price and quantity. The market equilibrium price allocates the production of a good to the producers who are the most cost-efficient and consumption of that good to the consumers who derive the most benefit or consumer surplus from their purchase. In the absence of market failure, this equilibrium will result in a pareto optimum, or socially efficient level of output. However, when market failure occurs, the level of output in the market will be greater than or less than the socially efficient level.

Frequently, the markets for information goods and services either suffer market failure or are created to correct for the inefficiencies that occur in some markets. Unlike other goods, information can be shared, jointly consumed, and can provide benefits or costs to those who are not direct consumers or producers. It is the lack of accurate information about quality medical care, automotive care, stock values, and other goods and services that often results in failure in these markets, making necessary the creation of markets for information.

Discussion Questions

1. Consider the effects of an increase in the cost of paper and ink on the supply of paperback books. What effect will this have on the market equilibrium price and quantity of sales?

2. What effect might the PBS series "The Civil War" have had on the demand for books on the Civil War? What effect might this demand have had on the market equilibrium price and quantity of books sold?

3. Library patrons receive books and services from public libraries without paying for them. In this case the librarian allocates library resources, purchases books and journals, and provides reference services based on the perceived demand for services. How efficient do you think this method is? Is it possible that a market failure might exist here? Explain.

4. Identify five markets for information goods or services that are created to supply information on the value or quality of other goods or services.

Note

1. Adam Smith, *An Inquiry into the Nature and Causes of the Wealth of Nations*, (New York: Oxford University Press, reprint of 1776 edition).

Part II

Market Failure and Information Markets

Externalities and Information Markets

5

Externalities occur when the production or consumption of a good generates benefits or costs to individuals other than the direct consumers or producers of that good. *Negative externalities* are social costs from the production or consumption of a good in excess of the direct costs of production. Pollution, damaging gossip, crowded roads, people talking in the library or movie theater, and excessive junk mail are all examples of negative externalities. In each case, a social cost is imposed on someone who is not directly determining consumption or production in the market. *Positive externalities* are social benefits from the production or consumption of a good or service in excess of the direct benefits in the market. Your neighbor's lawn care, public inoculations against infectious diseases, good news, and charitable contributions to nonprofit organizations are examples of positive externalities.

For both types of externalities, market prices, which connect buyers and sellers, do not factor in the external benefits or costs imposed on other members of society. For this reason, decisions made by consumers and producers do not reflect the full social benefit or cost of the good or service. As a result, the socially efficient level of output may be greater or less than the competitive market equilibrium.

Many information goods and services exhibit externalities. Often individuals do not want to read, see, or hear information such as junk mail, advertisements, sexually explicit material on television, bad news, others talking in the library, and so on, but they receive this information regardless of their wishes. In these examples, the consumption of individuals who purchase the products of advertising or want to receive the information cannot be separated from those who do not want to receive it. As a result, the consumption of the information by its consumers imposes a negative externality on those who do not want it.

Other times, information that may benefit others is not received by them. For example, information on the quality of products, class notes for the final exam, and other helpful information may or may not be given to all who could benefit from it. The direct consumers of this information, those who have researched the quality of a product or attended the class to take notes, do not always have the ability or incentive to share this information with others for whom it would be a positive externality.

Negative Externalities and Information Markets

Negative externalities are by-products of markets for goods or services. They are social costs produced as the result of market behavior but not incorporated into the decisions of producers and consumers participating in the market. When paint is produced and consumed, the negative externality of pollution is also produced. When travelers use roads for their personal benefit, they do not consider the social costs of traffic congestion on other travelers. When direct mail is sent to potential consumers, direct marketing firms also send junk mail to households uninterested in purchasing their products. When gossip is passed among friends, the friends rarely consider the negative externality their conversations may have on the subject of the gossip. When someone talks to a friend during a movie they seem unaware that they are annoying other patrons. In each case a social cost is imposed on someone who is not directly determining consumption or production in the market. As a result, the competitive equilibrium level of output of the good or service exceeds the socially efficient level.

An excellent example of a market with a negative externality is the market for direct marketing or junk mail. Direct marketing mail provides some people with useful information about available goods. But it is a negative externality to others who do not want to spend the time to review and discard it. This is the result of a market in which the individuals who pay for the junk mail and receive the most direct benefit from it, direct marketing firms, are not the individuals who receive it. The companies who produce the junk mail impose costs on others who are not paying for it or directly participating in the production or distribution of it.

The benefit direct marketing firms receive from junk mail is increased sales resulting from the advertising. The direct cost of junk mail, that considered by direct marketing firms, is the cost of paper and postage. So long as the expected benefit of increased profit to the owners of the direct marketing firm exceeds the cost of sending direct mail, these firms will produce and mail it. The level of junk mail sent will be determined by the expected marginal benefit by the direct marketing firms who pay for it, and will be only indirectly influenced by the individuals who receive the mail.

Figures 5.1 and 5.2 illustrate the marginal costs and marginal benefits of junk mail. The equilibrium level of junk mail, Q^*, is the intersection of the marginal cost (supply) curve (MC) and the marginal benefit (demand) curve (MB). This equilibrium is the level of junk mail that maximizes the direct marketing firm's profit. To maximize profit, a direct marketing firm will send out mail as long as the marginal benefit, or expected profit, from that mail exceeds the marginal cost of $0.30. For example, the Qth piece of mail gives an expected profit of $0.40 at a marginal cost of $0.30 for a net profit of $0.10. When the marginal benefit of the next mailing is less than the marginal cost, as occurs to the right of Q^*, the firm stops sending out additional mailings. Without loss of generality, it can be assumed that the additional profit from direct marketing decreases for each additional mailing; in other words, the marginal benefit curve for junk mail slopes downward (see fig. 5.3).

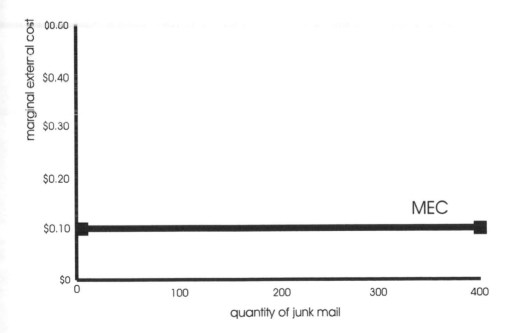

Figure 5.1. Marginal External Cost of Junk Mail.

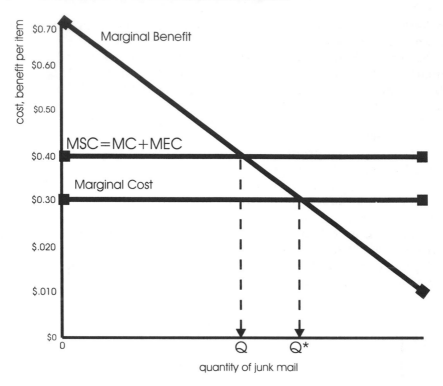

Figure 5.2. Equilibrium and Efficient Level of Junk Mail.

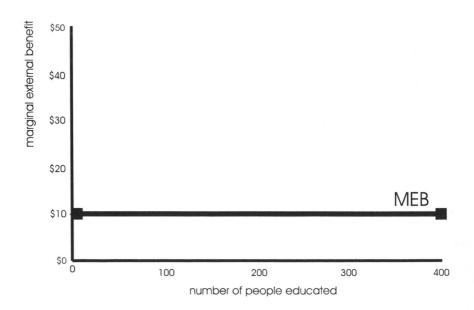

Figure 5.3 Marginal External Benefit of Sex Education.

However, direct marketing firms do not consider the social costs, or negative externality, imposed on consumers who must spend time discarding the junk mail. The cost of the externality can be approximated by measuring the cost of the time spent by individuals who involuntarily receive direct mail. Assume that every piece of junk mail takes 10 seconds to review, open, and discard. Also assume that the opportunity cost or value of time for the average person is $36 per hour; then the marginal external cost (MEC) of each piece of junk mail is $0.10 per piece (see fig. 5.1).

The financial cost, or marginal cost (MC), of junk mail to the direct marketing firm is the cost of labor and paper plus the cost of postage. Assume that this equals $0.30 per piece of junk mail. The cost to society per piece of junk mail is the *marginal social cost* (MSC), which equals the financial cost to the direct marketing firm plus the marginal external cost to individuals who receive it (MSC = MC + MEC). In our example, the marginal social cost of junk mail equals $0.40 per piece. These cost curves are shown in figure 5.2.

If the marginal social cost of the junk mail is considered, the total social cost is $0.40 per letter ($0.30 in mailing costs plus $0.10 of externality), not the $0.30 assumed by direct mailing firms. Therefore, the social optimum level of junk mail is Q, which is less than Q*. For all letters mailed between Q and Q* the marginal social cost of the letter exceeds the marginal benefit the direct marketing firm receives from it. Society (consumers and producers) would be better off if the junk mail between Q and Q* were not sent.

As in the example of the market for junk mail, information products that impose negative externalities are frequently overproduced. Producers and consumers are unlikely to consider the negative effects of their actions on others, particularly when profit or self-interest motivate actions, and external costs are difficult to observe. The dissemination of information, in the form of advertising, is also difficult to selectively target or consume. The direct marketing firms cannot effectively send out their catalogs and letters only to those individuals who will purchase their products. Similarly, individuals cannot open only those pieces of mail advertising products they want to purchase. Information must be consumed before its value, or cost, can be determined.

Positive Externalities and Information Markets

While negative externalities are social costs not considered by producers and consumers, positive externalities are social benefits from the production or consumption of a good or service in excess of the direct benefits received by consumers. Because the actual consumers of the good or service do not receive these external benefits, they are not expressed in the consumers' demand or willingness to pay for the good or service. As a result, consumers will purchase less of the good or service than is socially optimal. Inoculations for contagious diseases, education, your neighbor's lawn care, a good review of the book you recently wrote, and, for some individuals, even junk mail are all examples of positive externalities.

Education is a good example of a service with positive externalities. An education can benefit not only the individual receiving it but also others who benefit from having more educated members of society. Children in school are not committing crimes; educated adults make better citizens; and everyone benefits from talking and working with intelligent, informed people.

Figures 5.3 and 5.4 illustrate the positive externality of sex education to prevent infection by sexually transmitted diseases (STD). The market benefit from sex education is the benefit accrued by those individuals, the consumers, who, as a result of the education, do not contract a sexually transmitted disease. The positive externality is the benefit received by people who did not directly receive the education, but whose risk of being infected is reduced because there are fewer uneducated STD carriers.

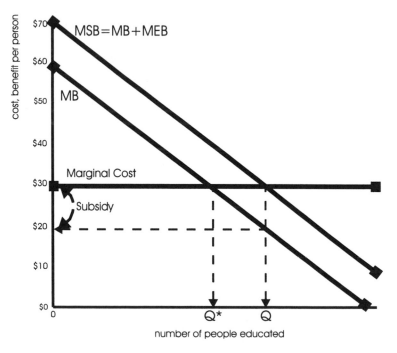

Figure 5.4. Equilibrium and Efficient Level of Sex Education.

Assume that the external benefit to people who don't take a sex education class averages $10 in saved medical bills and lost wages per each person educated about STDs. This average external benefit is the total cost in lost wages and medical bills divided by the total number of people who might come into contact with those who take the classes. This calculation is shown in appendix B (page 175). Figure 5.3 illustrates the positive externality, the marginal external benefit (MEB), to those who avoid becoming infected because their partners received this education.

There is also a cost to sex education. To simplify this example, assume that the costs of providing the education—the cost of printing pamphlets on safe sex—is trivial. In this case, that the marginal cost (MC) of sex education is the opportunity cost or value of the time individuals must spend to find and read the information (see fig. 5.4).

In figure 5.4, the marginal benefit curve (MB) illustrates the perceived benefit as a result of receiving an education about practicing safe sex. Individuals to the right of Q* find that the value of their time to educate themselves exceeds their expected value of the education. These individuals perceive that they are at a lower risk for infection than individuals represented to the left of Q*. (A more detailed discussion of how to calculate the costs and benefits of sex education is presented in appendix B, on page 175.)

The marginal social benefit (MSB) of sex education is the sum of the benefits to those who are educated (MD) plus the positive externality to their future partners (MEB). Therefore, the socially efficient level of sex education is at Q, where the actual benefit of sex education, the marginal social benefit, matched the costs of the education. Q, the socially efficient level of sex education, is greater than the market equilibrium at Q*. This is because individuals who receive education consider only the benefits to themselves, not the external benefits received by future partners or the subsequent partners of future partners who will not be infected. Therefore, fewer people will receive the education than is socially optimal.

Government Policy and Positive Externalities

Frequently, when there are positive externalities from the consumption of a good or service, the government provides subsidies, regulates the market, or imposes government mandates on services. In this example, government subsidies or government provision of sex education through the public schools may help increase the level of sex education to the socially efficient level. For example, as shown in figure 5.4, a subsidy of $10 will increase the level of sex education to the socially efficient level. A subsidy of $10 increases the number of people who are willing to take sex education classes. This $10 subsidy pays students the value of the marginal external benefit. However, the subsidy may not be a direct payment to students. This subsidy may take the form of mailing information to at-risk individuals or providing them with education at bars, hospitals, or other locations where the opportunity cost or value of time spent acquiring the literature will be lower than having to travel to a health care provider and ask for information.

Many information goods are provided or subsidized by the government to raise the output of these goods to the marginal social benefit when the market output is too low because it does not factor in positive externalities. Health and safety education, consumer information, and political information can all have positive externalities; however, the government provision or subsidy of these services is not without cost. While the existence of a positive externality implies an underprovision of these goods and services, a complete analysis of the need for government subsidies or provision requires calculating the cost of government involvement and comparing it to the benefit of correcting for the positive externality.

Balancing Positive and Negative Externalities

It is also possible for the consumption or production of information goods and services to have a positive externality on some people and a negative externality on others. For example, while some people feel that sex education prevents the spread of infectious diseases and lessens the incidence of teenage pregnancy, others feel that sex education encourages premature sex among teenagers. If sex education results in individuals who feel unjustifiably safe engaging in sexual behavior, it may impose a negative externality on others by resulting in unwanted pregnancy, the spread of a sexually transmitted disease, or emotional trauma from premature sexual behavior.

Junk mail, which has a negative externality on those who dislike it, has a positive externality on those recipients who enjoy it or find it useful. Some people simply enjoy receiving mail, regardless of its source. Others are consumers of the products advertised through direct mail and receive consumer surplus from their purchases. Because the consumer surplus is a benefit in excess of the profits or revenues received by the direct marketing firm, it is a positive externality. The marginal external benefit from those who enjoy junk mail and the consumer surplus from those who purchase the products advertised in junk mail are illustrated in figure 5.5 and figure 5.6.

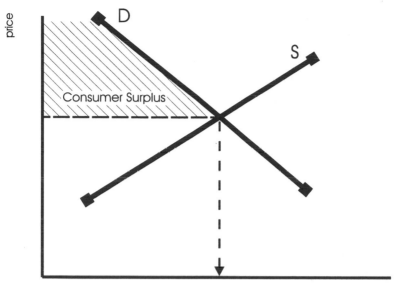

Figure 5.5. Consumer Surplus from Purchases Made Through Junk Mail.

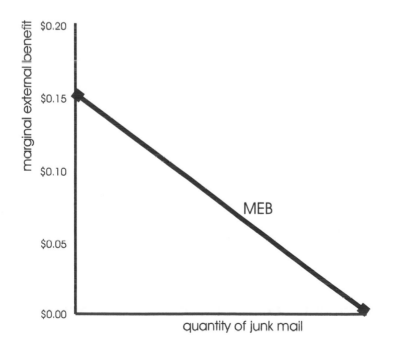

Figure 5.6. Marginal External Benefit of Junk Mail.

Figure 5.5 shows the consumer surplus received by buyers of the products sold through direct marketing. If one assumes that there is a direct relationship between the amount of junk mail and the purchases of these consumers—for example, each 100 pieces of mail may result in one item sold—then the consumer surplus from every item sold produces a positive externality for every 100 pieces of direct mail. This consumer surplus is not included in the profits of direct marketing firms as it is the benefit consumers receive over and above the amount they pay for their purchases. Figure 5.6 shows the marginal external benefit from the junk mail, which includes this consumer surplus, plus the external benefit to those who simply enjoy receiving mail. As the amount of junk mail increases, the expected purchases per 100 pieces declines as does the consumer surplus. Therefore, the marginal external benefit curve for junk mail is downward sloping.

The marginal benefit (MB) from junk mail is the profit received by producers from sales. The marginal benefit is added to the marginal external benefit to get the marginal social benefit curve in figure 5.7. Each piece of junk mail provides benefits to three groups—direct marketing firms, their consumers, and those who enjoy receiving mail—and costs to two groups—direct marketing firms and those who dislike junk mail. The socially efficient level of junk mail in figure 5.7 is Q, where the marginal social benefit from junk mail equals the marginal social cost from it. The socially efficient level of junk mail, Q, is less than the equilibrium level because the value of the negative externality (nuisance of junk mail) exceeds the value of the positive externality (consumer surplus from sales plus enjoyment of junk mail). However, if the value of the positive externality were to exceed the value of the negative externality, efficient government policy would be to subsidize the delivery of junk mail!

The result illustrated in figure 5.7 depends on the assumptions made about the marginal external costs and marginal external benefits from junk mail. If direct marketing firms could perfectly identify those individuals who want to receive junk mail and those who do not, then there would be no negative or positive externalities in this market. Direct marketing firms do not want to send junk mail to individuals who are annoyed by it because it is unlikely that they will become consumers of the products, and they could save mailing costs by removing them from their mailing lists. Similarly, if the firms could predict who would purchase the products advertised, they could send mail only to those households and, for the last piece of mail sent, the marginal cost of sending to that household would equal the marginal benefit or profit the firm would receive from it. At equilibrium, the consumer surplus of the last unit purchased would equal zero and there would be no positive externality. Unfortunately, direct marketing firms cannot perfectly predict which households want to receive mailings and which do not.

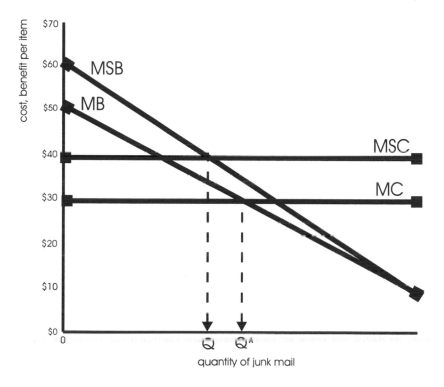

Figure 5.7. Equilibrium and Efficient Level of Junk Mail, Including Marginal Social Benefit.

Summary

As shown in the examples reviewed in this chapter, many information products and services have positive externalities, negative externalities, or both. When externalities are present, the socially efficient level of output will be different from the market equilibrium, resulting in market failure. In the case of negative externalities, the economically efficient level of output is less than the equilibrium level. In the case of a positive externality, the economically efficient level of output is greater than the socially efficient level. When both are present, the relative strengths of positive and negative externalities determine whether the socially efficient level is more, less, or equal to the market equilibrium.

Government policy may be able to correct market failures caused by externalities. With negative externalities, government regulation, taxes, or education programs that promote a reduction in the consumption of a good or service, such as unsafe sex, may decrease the level of output to the socially efficient level. With positive externalities, government subsidies, regulation, or education programs that promote the consumption of a good or service, such as health and safety, may increase the level of output to the socially efficient level.

Frequently, information goods and services either exhibit positive or negative externalities or promote the correction of a market failure. Because information can be shared at a relatively low cost, it can provide a benefit or cost to individuals other than those who originally purchased it. Because valued information can be used by individuals other than the purchaser, it has a positive externality, while false, slanderous, or negative information has a negative externality on those it affects. Negative and positive externalities can sometimes be corrected by educating market participants about their actions. Externalities resulting from pollution and unhealthy or unsafe behavior can be corrected by education, typically at a low cost relative to the social costs of the externality.

Discussion Questions

1. Many people believe that sex education in schools encourages promiscuity among young adults. If this is true, then sex education may have a negative externality. Discuss how this affects the socially optimal level of sex education. Is it possible that at the market equilibrium some groups receive too much education while others receive too little?

2. How is slander a negative externality? What does the government do to correct this market failure?

3. Surveys have shown that many people believe that condoms are 100% effective in preventing the spread of the HIV virus— the virus that causes AIDS—even though several scientific studies have shown that the prevention rate is far lower than this. Given this information, is it possible that minimum information can be a negative externality while complete information is a positive externality?

Information as a Public Good

Goods consumed by only one person are called *private goods*. For example, you may purchase a magazine or newspaper, read it, and then throw it away or purchase food, clothing, or other goods and services for your private consumption. In each of these examples you make an individual decision that the benefit you receive from that good is greater than the cost of it. However, some goods provide a benefit to more than one person.

Public goods are goods consumed by more than one person. This does not mean that the public good is produced by the public sector, only that the consumption is shared by more than one person. Books in the library, a television broadcast, a fireworks display, information, and a lecture are all public goods. More than one person enjoys benefits from each of these goods without significantly detracting from the consumption benefit enjoyed by others. The library book is used by more than one person in its lifetime. The television broadcast is viewed by hundreds of people. Information can be heard and used by several people simultaneously.

Public goods are non-rival in consumption. *Non-rival* means that more than one person can share the benefit of the consumption of the good. As a result of non-rival consumption, public goods are efficiently financed through the joint cooperation of consumers. A spectacular Fourth of July fireworks display is financed cooperatively by individual taxpayers in the community. Individuals who benefit from the consumption of the public good must each give or pay a fair share of the total revenues needed to support it. However, financing for public goods does not necessarily have to come from taxes. Financing of public goods can also occur through user fees, donations, or advertising revenues. For example, the production of information in a newspaper, which is collectively consumed by all readers, is financed through the price of the paper and through advertising revenues. A movie, jointly consumed by all patrons, is financed solely by user fees.

73

A network television broadcast is financed by advertising revenues, while public television and televangelists are financed by donations.

Many information goods are jointly consumed and financed. Newspapers, the information superhighway, books in a library, television broadcasts, telephone networks, and satellite transmissions are public goods, among other services. In each case, consumers collectively finance the production of the good and jointly share the consumption of it. The ability of producers to pay for the good through some method of finance determines whether the socially efficient level of the public good is attained. Because public goods must be jointly financed, it is not always possible to ensure that everyone who receives benefit from the consumption of the good contributes their fair share to finance it.

Social Efficiency

Chapter 4 showed that the socially efficient level of output of a private good occurs when the marginal benefit to consumers equals the marginal cost of production. However, unlike a private good, a public good's units of output provide benefits to many consumers simultaneously. Therefore, the benefit of each unit of a public good is not the benefit provided to one individual but rather the cumulative benefit provided to all those who consume it. The socially efficient level of output for a public good occurs when the sum of the benefits to all consumers equals the marginal cost of producing it. This is illustrated in table 6.1 and figure 6.1.

Table 6.1.
Marginal Benefits from the Information Superhighway.

Billions of Dollars Invested	Marginal Benefit per Unit per Year			
	Vince's	Geraldine's	Donna's	Total
1	$10	$15	$4	$29
2	$8	$10	$3	$21
3	$6	$5	$2	$13
4	$4	$0	$1	$5
5	$2	$0	$0	$2

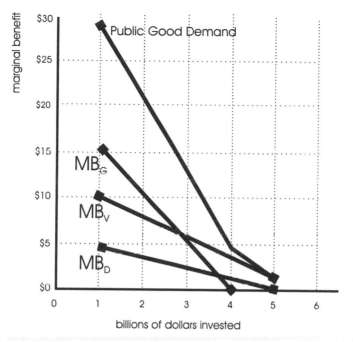

Figure 6.1. Marginal Benefits from the Internet.

Table 6.1 and figure 6.1 show Vince's, Geraldine's, and Donna's hypothetical marginal benefit from infrastructure investment in the national information superhighway. If a $1 billion annual investment is made in the Internet, Vince's use of the Internet would give him $10 in benefit per year, Geraldine's use would give her $15 in benefit, and Donna's use would give her $4 in benefit. In other words, if connect time to the Internet were sold, Vince would be willing to pay $10 a year for the amount of time he uses the Internet. Because each of these three individuals uses the same national network, the collective benefit from or willingness to pay for the first billion dollars of investment would be $29. The public good demand curve in figure 6.1 is the vertical sum of the individual marginal benefit curves for Vince, Geraldine, and Donna.

As investment increases, the quality of the connection to the Internet and the availability of resources on the Internet increases. For each one billion dollars of additional investment, Vince, Geraldine, and Donna receive additional benefits from their access to it. By assumption in table 6.1, the marginal benefits of each additional billion in investment decreases, and therefore the total benefit for each additional billion-dollar investment decreases.

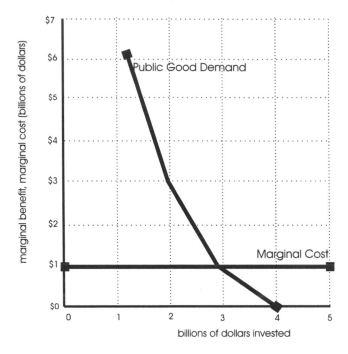

Figure 6.2. Efficient Investment in the Internet.

The public good demand curve for the national information superhighway is the collective benefit to all users—including Vince, Geraldine, and Donna—of the information superhighway. This is shown in figure 6.2. The hypothetical public good demand curve in figure 6.2 is the vertical sum of the marginal benefit curves of all individuals who use the Internet. The marginal cost of a one-billion-dollar investment in the Internet is simply one billion dollars. According to figure 6.2, for every billion dollars invested up to three billion dollars, the marginal social benefit from investment is greater than the marginal cost. If investment exceeds three billion dollars, the marginal social benefit is less than the marginal cost. Therefore the efficient level of investment in the Internet is three billion dollars. From this three-billion-dollar investment, Vince receives $24 ($10 + $8 + $6) in benefit, Geraldine receives $30 in benefit, and Donna receives $9 in benefit from their annual use of the Internet (see fig. 6.1).

Public good demand curves can be constructed for all goods that provide a collective benefit. However, unlike private goods for which consumers express their marginal benefit by purchasing the good, the marginal benefit or value of public goods must be estimated. In the case of the Internet, the level of use and the value of an individual's time spent using the Internet is one way to measure the marginal benefit individuals receive from it. Use statistics of public goods—such as the library, computer services, and public concerts—are collected to determine if the value to those who consume the public good exceeds the cost of providing it.

In 1984, Mathematica Corporation produced a report for the Securities and Exchange Commission that examined the potential benefits of a system designed to provide electronic access to corporate information filed with the SEC over the information superhighway.[1] Previously, investors and others interested in this information had to travel to one of the SEC distribution cities, ask for a copy of the SEC forms on a particular company, and photocopy those forms at the SEC office. The electronic system, coined EDGAR, provides electronic access to this information to anyone with a personal computer.

EDGAR is an example of a public good that provides a collective benefit to many investors and others interested in information from the SEC. To measure this benefit, Mathematica employees surveyed potential users of EDGAR, including institutional investors, corporations, and individual investors, and asked them to quantify the value of access to such a system. The survey asked the respondents how often they would use the system and how much they would be willing to pay for it. The amounts potential consumers were willing to pay were summed to estimate the collective benefit of the EDGAR system. In total, Mathematica Corporation estimated that the public good benefit of the EDGAR system would be approximately $2.3 billion per year.

Financing Public Goods

Exclusionary public goods, sometimes referred to as *club goods*, are those public goods from which individuals can be excluded, at a reasonable cost, from consuming or benefiting. This property enables these public goods to be financed in whole or part through user fees.

Movies are a common example of exclusionary public goods. *Citizen Kane* is a public good. It was produced for many consumers to enjoy over time. Some individuals consume it simultaneously with other viewers in a movie theater while others consume it by renting the video. All consumers benefited from its initial production. However, while the production of *Citizen Kane* or any other movie benefits all who view it, only those who pay the price of a ticket or rent the videotape can consume it. The exclusionary property of movies enables commercial producers to finance the supply of movies through user fees. Other examples of exclusionary public goods produced by the commercial or nonprofit sectors include cable television, private education, private clubs, and credit reports. Public swimming pools, toll roads, the EDGAR system, and public higher education are examples of exclusionary public goods produced by the public sector.

Table 6.2.
Examples of Public Goods.

	Provided by Federal, State, or Local Governments	Provided by Commercial or Nonprofit Organizations
Exclusionary	Toll roads, some national parks, public higher education, information	Movies, private education, credit reports, private clubs, amusement parks, cable television, information
Non-exclusionary	Fireworks displays, light-houses, some public parks, public roads, information	Broadcast television, radio, charitable contributions, information

Nonexclusionary public goods are those from which individuals cannot be effectively excluded. Examples of exclusionary and nonexclusionary public goods are shown in table 6.2. Examples of nonexclusionary public goods include fireworks displays, some public parks, many public roads, broadcast television, and radio. In each case, it is difficult or costly to exclude certain consumers from benefiting from the good. Local governments could post toll collectors at every road; however, the expense of doing this would exceed the revenues for many roads. Television programming could be offered only through cable systems, and might be in the future, but for now broadcast television is available to all who purchase a television set. Unlike exclusionary goods, for which user fees pay many of the costs of production, other financing must be used to pay for the production of nonexclusionary goods.

Exclusionary and nonexclusionary public goods can be financed by taxes, voluntary contributions, or revenues from other sources such as advertising. As a result, these goods are supplied by a variety of producers, including commercial firms; nonprofit organizations; federal, state, and local governments; and the collective actions of concerned individuals.

Nonexclusionary public goods are frequently supplied by governments and financed by taxes. Because of the nonexclusionary character of these goods, the only way to pay for their production is to make payment compulsory. A public road will be used by many members of the community; therefore, the community taxes all its members to pay to build and maintain the road. Many public finance economists believe that the primary responsibility of governments is to provide nonexclusionary public goods. However, while governments can collect taxes to pay for public goods, the problems of how much of the public good to provide, how much benefit citizens get from these public goods, and how much each citizen should be taxed are difficult to answer.

Public goods can be financed by donations. This method of finance, though, often results in a level of output less than the socially efficient level of output. When public goods are financed by voluntary contributions, such as public television and radio, the organization must rely on donors to make a fair assessment of the marginal benefit they receive from the public good and contribute this amount. However, donors may give less than their fair share or get a free ride by enjoying the public benefits of a good that has been financed by the donations of others. Donor free-riding results in less than the economically efficient level of the public good being produced. Frequently, nonprofit organizations exert social pressure on individuals to prevent free-riding. Public television and radio stations give out coffee mugs, books, and other items to reward those who pay their fair share, while donors to universities, museums, and other organizations will receive a recognition for their donation in a university newsletter or on a wall plaque.

Information as a Public Good

Information is a public good that can be exclusionary or nonexclusionary. An example of information as an exclusionary public good is medical research and development. Information on how to cure AIDS is a public good as the knowledge can be used to cure several patients simultaneously without decreasing the potential to cure others. While individuals will receive treatment as a private good (the service of a doctor), the knowledge of how to treat the disease is a public good.

The treatment or cure for AIDS or any other disease is an exclusionary public good because the law establishes the inventor as having an exclusionary right to his research. Inventors will file a patent on the cure and thereby establish it as their intellectual property; a consumer of this intellectual property must pay to benefit from that knowledge. This property right and the patent laws that enforce it establish an exclusionary mechanism to pay inventors for their time and effort in developing a cure. The exclusionary property of this type of information enables producers to invest in research and development in hopes of finding a cure. If they are fortunate enough to discover the cure, the protections will enable them to receive revenues, user fees, to cover their costs. However, these laws may also exclude some patients from receiving the cure if they cannot pay for it.

The property of exclusionarity does not imply that a public good must be financed through user fees, only that it can be financed in this way. The Internet, libraries, and public primary education are also exclusionary public goods, although they are usually not financed by user fees. Governments finance the production of public good through taxes. Other revenues include entrance fees, user fees, or tuition. Financial support for the Internet comes from tax revenues and user fees charged to universities, businesses, nonprofit organizations, and commercial companies such as Prodigy and CompuServe that sell access to individuals. While subscribers to a commercial service pay a fee for access, university users are not usually charged for use of the Internet.

Information can also be a nonexclusionary public good. For example, you can prevent the spread of diseases such as colds and flu by periodically washing your hands. Unlike a cure for AIDS, this information is a nonexclusionary public good. Even if someone was given the intellectual property right to this information, they would not be able to collect a fee every time this basic step for preventing infection was shared. Instead, the information spreads among those who benefit from it without payment to an inventor.

Some information goods financed by exclusionary sales are shared by consumers. Computer software is an example. Research into the development of a computer software program is an exclusionary public good. Copyright and patent law are used to enforce payment by consumers to the inventor for his time and effort. These laws create an exclusionary mechanism to finance further research and development in the computer software industry.[2]

Unfortunately, computer software is easy to copy and share with others. In spite of the laws protecting the intellectual property of creators, computer software piracy is extensive. It has been estimated that 33 percent of software on personal computers in the United States is illegally copied from a legally purchased copy, and software piracy rates are much higher in other countries. In this case, laws to enforce exclusionarity of a public good and ensure future financing are limited in their capacity for enforcement and their effectiveness in preventing some free-riding users from benefiting illegally from the public good.

Summary

Public goods are non-rival goods in consumption; they benefit many consumers. Because they are non-rival, financing must be shared among the consumers of the good. Information on the value of the good by individual consumers must be estimated to determine the economically efficient level of output and payment by individual consumers.

Information is a public good. It can be simultaneously consumed by more than one person without detracting from the consumption of others. As a result, many information goods and services must be financed by a collective mechanism. This can either be through donations, taxes, advertising, or, in the case of exclusionary information goods, through user fees. Copyright and patent laws enforce the exclusionarity of intellectual property to ensure an economically efficient level of research and development.

Discussion Questions

1. Comment on the following statement: "If a public good is exclusionary, it is best to leave its production to the private sector rather than the public sector." How does exclusionarity influence the ability of the private sector to finance the production of a public good?

2. Assume that your company has given you the authority to purchase either a local area network (LAN) for your staff or three additional printers. The cost of the LAN is $12,000; the printers cost $4,000 each. Assume that the LAN would be shared by everyone, but that each printer would be given to only one employee (i.e., the LAN is a public good but the printers are private goods). Table 6.3 shows estimates of increased productivity for each member of your staff for use of the LAN or printer.

Table 6.3.
Value of LAN and Printers to Employees.

Employee	Benefit from Community LAN (Public Good)	Benefit from Personal Printer (Private Good)
Butler	$2,000	$5,000
Fennema	$3,000	$4,000
Harrington	$500	$2,000
O'Rourke	$8,000	$6,000
Skaer	$2,000	$4,000

Should you purchase the LAN or the three printers? If you were to purchase the three printers, who should get them? If you did not have information on the value of each item to each employee, how might you estimate it?

3. Assume that the computer graphics software you and your colleagues want costs $500, but none of you can afford to purchase it. What illegal activity might you engage in to obtain a copy of this software? Is it possible that software piracy might increase the number of copies sold? Comment on the economic efficiency and ethics of this.

Notes

1. Myles Maxfield Jr., "Potential Impact of the Securities and Exchange Commission's EDGAR System on the Market for Securities Information" (Washington, DC: Mathematica Policy Research, 1984).

2. For a more detailed discussion of the economics of intellectual property law see Stanley M. Besen and Leo J. Raskind, "An Introduction to the Law and Economics of Intellectual Property," *Journal of Economic Perspectives* 5, no. 5 (1991): 3-28.

Monopolistic Pricing and Noncompetitive Markets

When sellers and buyers compete in the marketplace, the resulting market equilibrium is economically efficient. Chapter 4 showed that competitive markets result in an allocation such that the last unit bought has a marginal value to the buyer just equal to the marginal cost. In this market scenario, sellers are constrained from raising prices because they would lose their customers to the competition. As a result, suppliers sell until the marginal cost of the last unit sold equals the market price. The market price and quantity are determined by the force of the invisible hand, consumers and producers competing with each other, each acting in his own self-interest but collectively producing a market equilibrium price and quantity. Consumers and producers take the market price as given and as individuals do not have a measurable impact on it.

Noncompetitive markets occur when either suppliers or consumers can control the market price and quantity sold. Usually this happens when one supplier controls the selling price of a good. The supplier restricts output, which drives up the equilibrium price and increases profit. In this case, the equilibrium will be less than the socially efficient level of output.

The market for journal subscriptions is the best example of what some believe is a noncompetitive market. Librarians and scholars are justifiably upset with publishers who charge exorbitant prices. As journal prices increase, librarians must decide which journal titles to eliminate from the library's collection or which other aspects of the library's budget to cut. This is particularly frustrating when librarians understand that the actual cost of printing another copy of a journal (the marginal cost) is far below the price the library is charged for a subscription. Yet federal copyright law ensures that journal publishers retain monopolist rights over the information contained in the journals.

The market for journal subscriptions combines two parts of the economy, publishing (the producer) and libraries (the consumer), with very different philosophies about providing access to information. These philosophies conflict with each other; a profit-motivated publisher with exclusive rights to production of the good seems to have an unfair advantage over a librarian, who abides by the philosophy of free and open access to information. In the market for journal subscriptions libraries are unable to afford expensive journal subscriptions that may provide benefit to their faculty. By pricing journal subscriptions so far above their marginal costs, the costs of the journal to the consumer far outweigh the marginal benefit patrons would receive from that journal title. By definition, this implies a social inefficiency.

A *monopoly* is a market in which there is only one producer of a good or service. Because there is no competition from similar goods, the monopolist has exclusive control over price and supply and may be able to increase profit by charging exorbitantly high prices, thereby preventing the market from the socially efficient level of output. At the higher monopoly price, the marginal benefit to a consumer of an additional unit of output is greater than the marginal cost (in a market equilibrium, these values are the same), resulting in the market failing to reach the pareto optimum.

Sometimes two or more firms collude with each other to maximize profit by acting together as if they were one single monopolist. A *duopoly* is a market in which there are only two producers of a good. An *oligopoly* is a group of producers who control a market such that it is noncompetitive.

It is also possible to have a market in which the suppliers behave competitively while the consumers, or demanders, control price and output. Although less common, this imbalance can also lead to a socially inefficient level of output. A *monopsony* is a market with only one consumer. In any of these markets, either the consumer or suppliers control the market price and quantity, often setting a price or quantity of output that may not be in the best interests of society.

Monopolies are pervasive in information markets. Local telephone service, mail delivery, and, in many communities, local cable television service is controlled by a single company. In these cases the high fixed costs of entering the market is justification for a single firm making a profit within a market; there isn't sufficient room for a competing firm to enter. When this happens, the state or federal government often regulates the single firm to prevent consumers from being exploited. Perhaps the most famous monopoly was American Telephone and Telegraph's (AT&T) monopoly on long-distance telephone service, which, prior to the court-ordered breakup, was tightly regulated by the federal government. However, after other companies—MCI and Sprint—proved that they could compete with AT&T over the sale of long-distance services, federal regulations relaxed but were not eliminated entirely.

In addition to these service monopolies, patent and copyright law create monopolistic control over some information goods. These laws to protect intellectual property rights also create sole providers of information and, as a result, create monopolies over books, journals, music, cures for diseases, new product lines, and other goods. In each case, efficient patent and copyright law must balance the protection of intellectual property against the economic efficiencies of a competitive market.

Monopolies

If there is more than one supplier of a product, it is difficult for an individual firm to increase price without losing customers to the competition. However, when monopolists control the supply of a good, they can increase price above the competitive market price without the fear of losing customers to the competition. This price increase pushes the market to a lower level of output than is socially efficient.

The basics of monopolies can be illustrated with a simple example. In many communities, local phone installation is provided through a government-regulated single supplier or local monopoly. Consider what your local phone company might charge for phone installation if its price was not regulated. This is shown in figure 7.1.

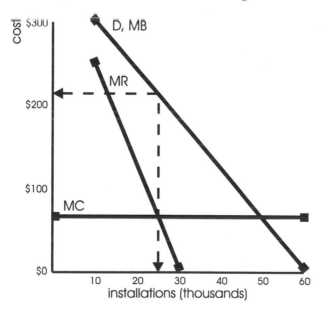

Figure 7.1. Monopoly Price and Output of Local Phone Company.

For simplicity, figure 7.1 assumes that the marginal cost (MC) of installing a phone is the same as the average cost ($75 per installation). This considers only the costs of the installation and lumps fixed costs into the cost of service. The $75 installation cost includes the cost of the wire, jacks, and other materials and also the labor of a telephone employee coming to one's home to install the phone. The demand (D) or marginal benefit (MB) curve for individuals who are willing to pay for a phone installation is also shown in figure 7.1 and the first two columns of table 7.1.

If phone installation was a competitive market, then the marginal cost curve (MC) in figure 7.1 would represent the market supply curve. In a competitive market, competition among firms would cause the market equilibrium price to settle at $75 per installation with 50,000 phones installed per year. Each firm would make exactly the marginal cost of an installation and would receive zero profit. If any firm attempted to increase its price to increase profit, they would lose all of their market share to firms that continued to charge $75.

The area above the marginal cost and below the demand curve is the consumer surplus in a competitive market. Consumer surplus is left to consumers in a competitive market because individual firms are prevented, by market forces, from increasing price above the equilibrium. However, a profit-maximizing monopolistic firm will extract this surplus from consumers to increase profit. Maximum profit is essentially the most revenue that can be taken from what would be consumer surplus in a competitive market.

Using the above example, if the local phone company was an unregulated monopoly it would raise the price of an installation to increase profit. Profit-price combinations are shown in table 7.1.

Column 5 of table 7.1 shows that the company maximizes profit by setting the price at $225 per installation and selling 25,000 installations. Column 6 is the *marginal revenue* (MR) from an installation, or the change in revenue, $\Delta(PQ)$, divided by the change in installations sold, ΔQ, as a result of the price being lowered. The marginal revenue is the additional revenue the producer expects to receive when the price is lowered and one more unit of output is sold. Column 6 shows that the profit-maximizing quantity is also the quantity such that the marginal revenue from an installation is about equal to the marginal cost. If one were to calculate the marginal revenue from an increase in demand of 24,999 to 25,000 one would observe that the marginal revenue is $75 for the 24,999th installation, exactly equal to the marginal cost. A monopolist will increase price until the additional revenue from selling one more installation, the marginal revenue (MR), equals the additional cost of the installation, the marginal cost.

Table 7.1.
Demand for and Profit from Phone Installation.

Demand Q (Thousands) (1)	Price P (2)	Revenue P•Q (Thousands) (3)	Cost MC•Q (Thousands) (4)	Profit P•Q- MC•Q (Thousands) (5)	Marginal Revenue Δ(P•Q)/ ΔQ (6)
20	$255	$5100	$1500	$3600	
23	$237	$5451	$1725	$3726	$117
25	$225	$5625	$1875	$3750	$87
28	$207	$5796	$2100	$3696	$57
30	$195	$5850	$2250	$3600	$27
35	$165	$5775	$2625	$3150	-$15
40	$135	$5400	$3000	$2400	
45	$105	$4725	$3375	$1350	
50	$75	$3750	$3750	$0	
Quantity demanded, Q= -(500/3)P + 62,500					

As illustrated in figure 7.2, the monopolist's pricing policy results in a level of output less than the socially efficient level of output. For each installation between 25,000 and 50,000, the marginal benefit to a consumer exceeds the marginal cost of the installation. For example, the 30,000th installation has a marginal benefit of $195 to a consumer and a marginal cost of only $75. This means there are $120 of net benefits that society could receive if this consumer was allowed to purchase an installation at cost. However, if the monopolist is restricted to charging only one price in this market or cannot discern between consumers and therefore must charge all consumers the same price, the monopolist will lose profit. As a result, all net benefits between the 25,000th installation and the 50,000th installation are lost to society. This social loss, called *deadweight loss*, equals the shaded area in figure 7.2.[1] The deadweight loss is the consumer surplus that society could have received if the price were set equal to $75.

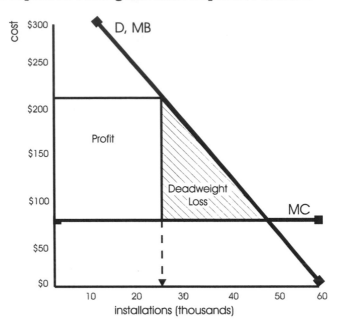

Figure 7.2. Social Loss from Monopolistic Pricing of Phone Installation.

Diagrams similar to figure 7.1 and figure 7.2 can be drawn for all noncompetitive markets. In each case, as firms are able to push prices above and output below the competitive market equilibrium, profits are gained at the expense of economic efficiency. Consumers with a lower marginal willingness to pay will be excluded from the market to increase monopoly profits.

Decreasing Average Costs and Natural Monopolies

Although monopolies can be extremely profitable, monopolies are difficult to maintain. When one firm is making significant profits, entrepreneurs and competitors are likely to enter the market. Monopolies are more likely when either the government ensures their existence through regulation or the structure of costs is such that one large supplier is likely to dominate the market. Many information goods and services have one or both factors working to create a monopolistic market.

In an industry with high fixed costs, declining average costs may result in a *natural monopoly*. A natural monopoly occurs when a firm must make a large fixed investment to enter the industry and marginal costs are low compared with this fixed investment. As output increases, average cost per unit decreases. As a result, a large single supplier can sell output at a lower price and drive out potential competitors. Public utilities, local telephone service, and cable companies are common examples of potential natural monopolies. In each case there is a large fixed investment of a network of telephone, cable, electric, fiber-optic, or gas lines along with a fixed investment of the power plant, cable company, or telephone switchboard. Compared with these fixed investments the cost of connecting one additional user is low.

Figure 7.3, which shows the cost curves for cable service, assumes that the fixed investment for a cable network is $2 million while the marginal cost of a connection is $20 per household.

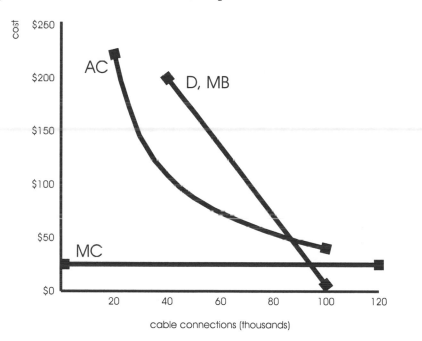

Figure 7.3. Natural Monopolies and Declining Average Costs for Cable Service.

Given the large fixed costs of the cable network and the relatively lower marginal cost of a connection, the average costs for a cable company decline over time. The larger a single cable company becomes, the lower the average cost of connecting an additional home. As a result, one large firm can drive prices lower than any smaller firm can match. Under our assumptions, the fixed investment of $2 million is simply too large for the market to support two competing firms.

In this case, the market equilibrium is for one large cable company to dominate service in the market. As a result, that firm can set price at a level just low enough to discourage smaller firms from competing with it yet high enough to make a profit. In the absence of government regulation, the price will be greater than the average cost or break-even price and less than or equal to the single-price monopolist's price, where marginal revenue equals marginal cost. Because the resulting price will be above the marginal cost, $20, there will be deadweight loss in this market. While the cost of connecting an additional consumer to the network would be only $20, the cable company is unwilling to lower its price.

Books, journals, software, and other electronic and print products frequently have downward sloping average cost curves. The large fixed investments for an individual book title or journal issue are the "first-copy" costs. For a book, first-copy costs include the author's time and the publisher's set-up costs of editing and printing the first copy. The marginal cost is the additional cost for printing, binding, and shipping one more copy of the book. Noll and Steinmueller (1992) analyze the declining average costs in the production of academic journals.[2] For electronic products, the first-copy costs include the time of the programmer and other fixed costs. The marginal cost is the additional cost of copying, packaging, and shipping one more copy of the program.

Although print and electronic products have downward sloping average cost curves, they are not natural monopolies. This is because while the initial production of a book or software program requires a large fixed investment, it is possible, for those willing to violate copyright law, to make copies at a low marginal cost. Illegal competitors need only a photocopy machine or personal computer to make copies for sale. These competitors do not have the same high fixed or first-copy costs of the original publisher. In the absence of laws protecting intellectual property, no publisher, author, or inventor would be willing to create intellectual property, because they would not receive a fair market return for their time and effort.

Patent and copyright laws protect the intellectual property of authors and inventors. However, in protecting these rights, these same laws create monopolies over specific products. Patent and copyright laws enable the owners of intellectual property to be the sole suppliers of that property. The author is the owner of the expression of the ideas contained in this book. As the owner, the author passes on his ownership to the publisher who in turn becomes the monopolistic supplier of this book. Copyright law ensures that this monopoly is maintained for the author's lifetime plus 50 years. Patent law enforces similar monopoly rights over a shorter period, usually 15 years, for inventions.

The problem of compensating individuals for their intellectual property and monopoly pricing is illustrated in figure 7.4 and figure 7.5. Figure 7.4 is the market for intellectual output (books, computer software, pharmaceutical drugs, or any other output protected by copyright or patent law). The quantity, Q, in figure 7.4 is the number of copies of a book, number of copies of a computer software program, number of prescriptions written for a particular pharmaceutical drug. The demand (MB) curve in figure 7.4 is the lifetime marginal benefit to consumers of this good. The creator's ability to exploit this market (the price charged), depends on the length of the patent or copyright, the breadth of copyright (i.e., how restrictive it is of similar products by other firms), and the value of the good or service to consumers. Assume that the initial price that maximizes profit for the copyright owner is P. This price results in a deadweight loss equal to area ABC.

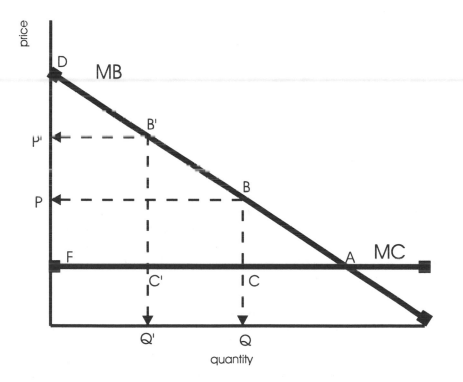

Figure 7.4. The Market for the Output of Intellectual Property.

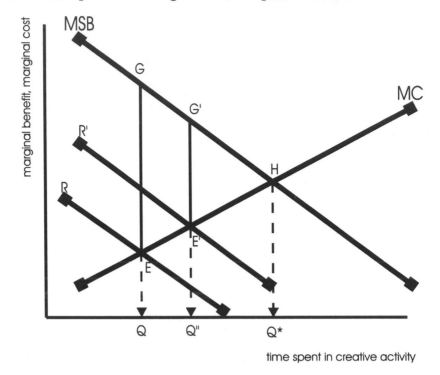

Figure 7.5. The Market for Creativity.

Figure 7.5 illustrates the market for creativity. The supply or marginal cost (MC) of creative endeavors is the cost of authors' or inventors' time and effort in writing books and computer programs and creating new pharmaceutical drugs. The marginal social benefit curve (MSB) in figure 7.5 represents the maximum net benefit possible from a given creative activity. This is the maximum consumer surplus possible if the output of this creative activity were sold at its marginal cost. The net benefit possible in figure 7.4 is area ADF, the maximum consumer surplus. Each creative endeavor has a cost equal to the time and effort of the inventor or author, and a potential benefit equal to the consumer surplus of the consumers of the goods that are created.

The line R in figure 7.5 is the expected profit line possible for creators. Expected profits from creative activity are less than the marginal benefit because not all consumer surplus can be transferred into profit. Given the expected profit from creative activity (R) and the marginal cost (MC) of time and effort by authors and inventors, there is an equilibrium in figure 7.5 at point E, where t hours are spent creating intellectual property. However, because inventors do not consider the consumer surplus from their endeavors, t is less than the socially efficient number of hours, t*. All hours employed in creating new books, drugs, and computer programs between t and t* hours would result in a potential consumer surplus greater than the cost of the authors' and inventors' hours. The resulting deadweight loss is represented by area EGH in figure 7.5.

To improve social efficiency in figure 7.5, additional profit must be made by creators of intellectual property. This may be possible by strengthening the copyright and patent laws to further protect intellectual property rights. As a result, higher profits are possible, represented by a shift from profit line R to R', and an increase in the hours devoted to creative activity from t to t'. Deadweight loss in figure 7.5 declines from area EGH to E'G'H.

However, stronger intellectual property laws increase the monopolistic exploitation possible by authors and inventors shown in figure 7.4. Stronger laws may take the form of lengthening the period of time over which copyrights and patents can be enforced, strengthening the legislation against substitute goods, or increasing the enforcement of existing laws to prevent illegal copying of intellectual property. As a result, stronger laws enable creators to increase the price on output from P to P', lowering the number of units of output sold from Q to Q', and increasing the deadweight loss from ABC to AB'C'. While the number of hours and effort in creative endeavor increases, lowering deadweight loss, the amount of output of any individual creation may decrease, increasing deadweight loss.

Optimal intellectual property right laws must balance the compensation of creators with the benefits to consumers. While strengthening laws increases creative effort, it also increases the capacity for monopolistic exploitation. Conversely, while weaker copyright laws offer consumers greater access to information through lower prices and substitute products, they decrease the time and effort spent by authors and inventors and may decrease the quality of creative output. A partial solution to this problem is to allow producers to charge different prices to different consumers or groups of consumers for the same good. Multi-price suppliers are able to extract a greater amount of consumer surplus as profit and are therefore given a greater financial incentive to engage in creative efforts.

Multi-Price Suppliers

Products are frequently sold to different consumers at different prices. Senior citizens receive discounts on goods and services; students, faculty, and libraries pay different prices for the same journal subscription; and businesses and educators pay different prices for the same computer software. Some readers pay for the first edition of a book in hardcover, while others wait for the lower-priced paperback or used copies to appear at their local bookstore.

This price differentiation allows suppliers to make greater profits by differentiating among consumers. If a supplier can segment consumer demand, the supplier can maximize profit over each demand segment. The result is a level of profit greater than can be achieved with a single price. The example of journal publishing can be used to illustrate this. Figure 7.6 shows the cost and demand curves for the fictitious *The Economists' Journal.*

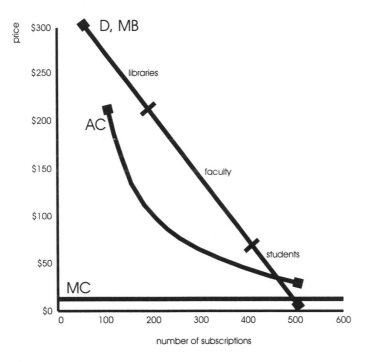

Figure 7.6. Multi-Price Monopolist and Segmented Markets for Journal Subscriptions.

The demand curve (D, MB) is divided into three segments: the library, faculty, and student demand for *The Economists' Journal.* Libraries are located along the entire length of the demand curve; however, most of the higher demand along the first segment of the demand curve constitutes demand by libraries. Large research libraries have more resources and are able to pay more for a journal subscription than any individual subscriber. In addition, a library's subscription can be viewed as a public good for many patrons so that the sum of their marginal willingness to pay for the subscription is larger than the willingness to pay by any individual subscriber. Faculty may also be located along the entire length of the demand curve; however, faculty demand will be concentrated within the middle segment.

Faculty have greater income than students but more limited resources than university libraries. The final segment of the demand curve will include most of the students in economics. These students have a lower willingness to pay for an economics journal because they have more limited resources than faculty and libraries. Of course, there are several other factors that influence library, faculty, and student willingness to pay for *The Economists' Journal*, including tastes, availability of the journal in the university library, and the number of faculty and students in the Economics Department.

The publisher of this or any other journal can maximize profits by selling subscriptions to the different groups of consumers at different prices. The publisher maximizes profit by segmenting the market into the libraries, faculty, and student groups and charging a different profit-maximizing price to each market segment. This is shown in figure 7.7.

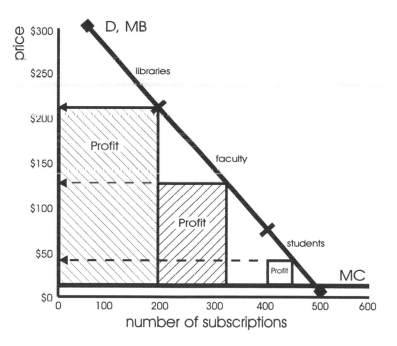

Figure 7.7. Multi-Price Profit Maximization for Journal Subscriptions.

Profit is maximized by setting prices such that marginal revenue is equal to marginal cost (MC) in each market segment. In this example, the publisher charges libraries a price of $220 for a subscription, faculty a price of $110, and students a price of $40. Libraries purchase approximately 200 subscriptions, faculty purchase an additional 160 subscriptions, and students purchase an additional 40 subscriptions. Profit is revenues minus the cost of printing and mailing the subscriptions sold in each of the three market segments and the fixed cost—or first copy cost—of production.

Multi-price publishers or monopolists can carve out a larger piece of consumer surplus than if they charged a single, common price to all consumers. Profit is maximized over each market segment, producing a higher total profit than maximizing profit using one price over the entire demand curve. With a single-price monopolist, all consumers would have to pay the same high price and, as a result, consumers with a lower willingness to pay—faculty and students—would be prevented from participating in the market. However, with the ability to segment the market, the price can be lowered for groups with lower demand, thereby enabling the publisher to extract additional profit over the low-demand segments.

For price discrimination to work effectively, consumers must be clearly identified into different market segments. In addition, consumers who purchase the good at a lower price must be prevented from making a profit by reselling the good in the high-demand market segments, undercutting the monopolist.

Haley and Talaga (1991) present the conditions necessary for price discrimination to work in the market for academic journals.[3] Chressanthis and Chressanthis (1993) provide evidence of this price discrimination.[4] In the market for journals, publishers can charge faculty and students lower prices without much concern that these groups will resell journals to the library. The increased reliance on journal donations and interlibrary loan of journal articles, however, noted by Haley and Talaga, is evidence of an attempt to circumvent the publishers' prices in the high-demand segment.[5] While the library subscription price is higher than individual subscription prices for many potential individual subscribers, the cost of photocopying a journal article at the library may be lower than the individual subscription price. Kingma and Eppard (1992) noted that library photocopying of journal articles by faculty and students is an effective mechanism for reselling the library subscription.[6] As a result, the journal subscription market produces the unusual circumstance in which consumers in the high-demand market segment resell the good to consumers in the low-demand segment. Liebowitz (1985) argues that publishers might be able to appropriate these photocopy revenues by increasing the price discrimination between libraries and individual subscribers.[7]

It should be noted that while a multi-price supplier extracts more consumer surplus into profit, the market equilibrium is closer to the socially efficient level of output than a single-price monopolist's level of output. In figure 7.7 the socially efficient level of output is at 500 subscriptions, the multi-price monopolist sells 400 subscriptions, while the single-price monopolist would sell only 250 subscriptions or roughly half of what is socially optimal. In fact, if the monopolist could specify a price for each individual consumer, the seller would charge each consumer their marginal willingness to pay and extract all of the potential consumer surplus as profit. In the end, the market equilibrium level of output would be the same as a competitive market equilibrium and the socially efficient level. However, society would receive all of the net social benefit in the form of profits rather than consumer surplus.

Summary

The high fixed costs and low marginal costs of reproduction cause many information goods and services to have declining average-cost curves. While this might result in a natural monopoly, the low marginal cost of reproduction prevents the owners of intellectual property from exploiting these markets because competitors can purchase one unit of the good and sell copies at a price lower than the authors' or inventors' average cost. Copyright and patent laws protect the intellectual property rights of authors and inventors, enabling them to receive compensation for their time and effort and encouraging future creative endeavors. Unfortunately, copyright and patent laws also enable suppliers of intellectual property to behave like monopolists and charge socially inefficient prices.

The social inefficiencies caused by monopolists depend on their ability to price-discriminate, on the regulatory environment, and on the closeness of substitutes for their products. Perfect price-discriminating monopolists can achieve the socially efficient level of output; however, all societal benefits from this output become monopoly profits rather than consumer surplus.

Discussion Questions

1. While copyright law ensures monopoly rights, it also ensures that authors are compensated for their creativity. Is it possible to balance these two competing interests? Explain.

2. Under current copyright law, authors and their descendants have copyright on intellectual property for the life of the author plus 50 years. Under current patent law, inventors have control over their work for 15 years. Why is there a difference? What does the length of protection have to do with pricing, competition, and importance of these different types of goods?

3. Fair use allows copying of copyrighted material for educational and newsworthy use. This enables you to make a photocopy of a journal article for a class without having to pay a copyright fee to the publisher. Without fair use, libraries would probably have to remove their photocopy machines because it would be impossible to enforce copyright. What effect would eliminating fair use have on the prices publishers charge libraries, faculty, and students for journal subscriptions?

4. Electronic journals accessible over the Internet are increasing in popularity every day. The electronic environment dramatically decreases the cost of copying the intellectual property of someone else. In paper form, you spend a few minutes and a few dollars to photocopy a journal article, while in electronic form a copy can be produced in a few seconds with a few keystrokes. What impact does this have on the ability of electronic authors to receive compensation for their intellectual property? How might this affect the quality of print versus electronic journals?

Electronic journal publishers have recently tried to implement user charges to raise revenues. How does the ease of reproduction affect the ability of publishers of electronic journals to implement user fees?

Notes

1. For a discussion of deadweight loss resulting from monopolies in the market for academic journals see David W. Lewis, "Economics of the Scholarly Journal," *College & Research Libraries* 50, no. 6 (November 1989): 674-88; and Bruce R. Kingma and Philip B. Eppard, "Journal Price Escalation and the Market for Information: The Librarian's Solution," *College & Research Libraries* 53 (1992): 523-35.

2. Roger Noll and W. Edward Steinmueller, "An Economic Analysis of Scientific Journal Prices: Preliminary Results," *Serials Review* 18, nos. 1-2 (1992): 32-37.

3. Jean Walstrom Haley and James Talaga, "Marketing Theory Applied to Price Discrimination in Journals," *The Journal of Academic Librarianship* 16, no. 6 (1991): 348-50.

4. George A. Chressanthis and June D. Chressanthis, "The Relationship Between Manuscripts Submission Fees and Journal Quality," *The Serials Librarian* 24, no. 1 (1993): 71-86.

5. Jean Walstrom Haley and James Talaga, "Academic Library Responses to Journal Price Discrimination," *College & Research Libraries* 53 (1992): 61-70.

6. Kingma and Eppard, "Journal Price Escalation and the Market for Information: The Librarian's Solution," 1992.

7. Stanley J. Liebowitz, "Copying and Indirect Appropriability: Photocopying of Journals," *Journal of Political Economy* 93, no. 5 (October 1985): 945-57.

Imperfect Information

Uninformed or misinformed consumers and producers tend to make poor decisions about a product's value. As a result, they are reluctant to buy or sell goods and services, and the market is unable to reach a socially efficient level of output.

Information markets are, by definition, susceptible to this problem because information consumers cannot test the quality of the books, magazines, movies, videotapes, or legal or consulting services they want until after they have bought them. They buy a book without fully knowing the quality of the authorship or the services of a lawyer without knowing in advance how valuable those services will be. For each of these goods and services, however, there are market mechanisms to correct for imperfect information. Book and movie reviews help determine the value of a book, movie, or videotape. Reading a current issue of a particular magazine provides a basis upon which to predict the quality of future issues. Remedial legal action can be pursued if the consulting services paid for are substandard. Professional association membership, the testimony of previous clients, and the provider's education and experience are all clues to the quality information consumers can receive.

Specific information markets have evolved specifically to correct for problems of imperfect information. Consumer magazines, movie reviews, legal guides, reputation, and word-of-mouth advertising all result from consumers' need to know about the quality of a good or service. Credit reporting agencies, medical history and doctor exams, and employee-provided references are information markets designed to help suppliers of credit, insurance, or jobs become better informed about their potential clients, customers, or employees.

Used Cars and Social Inefficiency

The problem of imperfect information becomes more pronounced if one side of the market has more information than the other. A classic example of asymmetrical information is the market for used cars, first examined by Akerlof (1970).[1] The seller of a used car generally has more information about the quality of the car than the buyer. Sellers know how well the car starts in the winter, the last time the brakes were replaced, the age of the muffler, the location of rust spots covered by paint, and a mechanic's opinion of the engine. Buyers can only guess at the car's quality. They can kick the tires, examine its miles and age, take a test drive, and check the engine; but much of their information (or misinformation) comes from the seller, who has an incentive to misrepresent the car's quality to the buyer. If the seller can convince the buyer that the used car is of higher quality than it appears, the seller can get a better price for his car.

Just as the seller has an incentive to misrepresent the quality of a used car, the buyer recognizes this and is suspicious of anything the seller says. As a result, the buyer discounts what she is willing to pay for a car by the probability the seller is misrepresenting the quality of the car to her. The buyer may be willing to pay only $5,000 for a car worth $6,000 simply because she cannot trust the seller to be honest.

Because all reasonably intelligent buyers assume sellers are misrepresenting the quality of their cars, sellers with high-quality used cars cannot sell them for what they are worth. The higher the quality of a used car, the more difficult it becomes to get paid what it is worth as potential buyers will be suspicious of its value. As a result, few high-quality used cars are sold, even though there may be buyers willing to buy them and sellers willing to sell them. The presence of, and assumption of, imperfect information in the used-car market prevents transactions between high-quality sellers and high-quality buyers.

Figure 8.1 illustrates the effects of imperfect information on the market for used cars. MB is the marginal benefit used-car buyers want to receive from their purchases. To illustrate the heterogeneity of used-car buyers, the marginal benefit for each buyer is ranked from lowest to highest, or from buyers interested in purchasing low-quality used cars to buyers interested in purchasing high-quality used cars (previous marginal benefit or demand curves ranked them from highest to lowest). The marginal benefit of the first buyer, or buyer of the lowest-quality used car, is $1,000. The marginal benefit of the last buyer in figure 8.1 is $4,500 for a used car. Sellers of used cars are ranked from those with the lowest-quality used cars to those with the highest-quality used cars along the supply curve S. If buyers can determine the quality of a used car, buyers—MB—and sellers—S—will match up with each other. Buyers looking for low-quality used cars will find sellers of low-quality used cars, while buyers of higher-quality used cars will match up with sellers of higher-quality used cars. The price paid for each used car will be somewhere between the marginal benefit a buyer expects to receive from the car and the seller's supply price. For example, the lowest-quality used car in figure 8.1 is worth $1,000 to a buyer while the seller is willing to supply it for $500. The actual price paid will be greater than $500 and less than $1,000 and will depend on the negotiating skills of the buyer and seller.

In the market, Q used cars will be sold. Buyers interested in used cars of higher quality than Q cannot find sellers who are willing to part with their high-quality used cars at a lower price.

Because used-car buyers do not know with certainty the quality of a car, they expect a level of benefit less than MB. For example, if buyers received a benefit or value of $4,000 from a "good" used car, but believed that there was a 10 percent chance that the car was a dud or that there is something wrong with the car, then the value they expect will be less than $4,000. If buyers believed that there was a 90 percent chance that the car was worth $4,000 and a 10 percent chance that the car was worth $0, then the expected benefit or value of the used car would be $3,600 [(0.9 x $4,000) + (0.10 x $0)]. Buyers will discount their willingness to pay by the chance that the used car is a dud. The curve MB' in figure 8.1 represents buyers' expected marginal benefits from used cars.

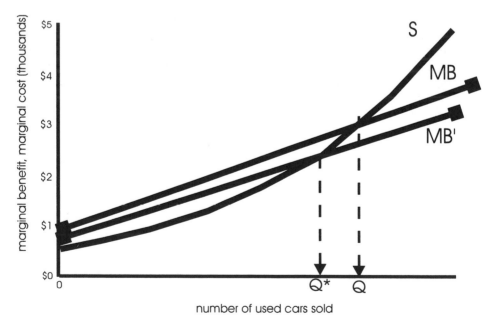

Figure 8.1. The Market for Used Cars.

Without perfect information, Q^* is the number of used cars sold. However, Q is the socially efficient level of used car sales. Owners of used cars between Q and Q^* have priced their product relatively high, because they perceive their cars as high-quality used cars. While some used car buyers have a benefit, MB, that is greater than the price at which sellers between Q and Q^* are willing to sell their cars, the asymmetry of information in this market prevents these transactions from occurring. Buyers are unwilling to trust sellers enough to believe that their cars are as high a quality as sellers advertise them to be. In markets with imperfect information, high-quality goods become more difficult to sell because buyers are reluctant to trust sellers.

Although markets with imperfect information can result in inefficiencies, there are also market corrections for these inefficiencies. If buyers can acquire sufficient information about the value of goods, then market inefficiencies can be mitigated to some degree. Studying consumer magazines and taking the car to a mechanic are ways buyers can acquire more information. Inefficiencies can also be resolved if sellers offer proof of product quality. Sellers of high-quality used cars may provide prospective buyers with detailed service and maintenance records or with the name of their mechanics to convince buyers of the value of the car. Sellers may also offer money back warranties if problems arise within a limited time period. The warranty may never be enforced but serves to reassure the consumer of the quality of the good.

The problem of imperfect information is prevalent in many, if not all, markets to varying degrees. Markets that suffer from imperfect information include new as well as used cars, electronic goods, computer software, stocks and bonds, health care, and over-the-counter and prescription drugs. In each case, the supplier or producer of the good has an incentive to misrepresent it as higher quality than it may actually be because consumers cannot accurately judge its value until after it has been purchased and used. As a result, consumers of these goods have a natural distrust of sellers. Market solutions to imperfect information include warranties, guarantees, good reputations, and name brands. Warranties and guarantees offer an additional contract to the buyer that ensures the quality of the good. Good product reputations and established name brands help ensure quality based on a historical record of quality. Low-quality producers who repeatedly misrepresent the quality of their goods to consumers are unable to attract repeat buyers, develop bad reputations, and ultimately go out of business. Good reputations—gained from years of selling high-quality, reliable products—give a positive signal to potential customers.

Nonprofit organizations can also represent their goods or services as being of higher quality than they really are. Child care, nursing home care, and help for the underprivileged or indigent are all examples of goods for which it is difficult to determine quality. Parents may investigate the quality of a child care agency, but they cannot remain with their child to observe the actual quality of care their child gets. When you make a contribution to the Salvation Army or American Red Cross, it is difficult to observe the quality of the services your donation pays for. If these services were provided by commercial organizations with the explicit goal of making a profit, it is likely that the quality of service might be reduced to increase profits. However, because these services are provided by nonprofit organizations, with a goal of providing high-quality service and not a goal of increasing profits, consumers and donors to these organizations feel they can trust the stated quality of services provided.

Solutions to markets with asymmetric information frequently come from within the market. Sometimes, though, government intervention is necessary to ensure that uninformed consumers are protected. Such government regulations include product-safety laws, false-advertising laws, and "lemon" laws. In New York State, "lemon laws" prevent car dealers from selling poor-quality cars that break down within the first 90 days after purchase. Government regulations also include certification for doctors, lawyers, plumbers, teachers, and other professionals. The Food and Drug Administration (FDA) regulates prescription and nonprescription drugs in an attempt to prevent consumers of medicines from purchasing low-quality or dangerous drugs that do not provide the benefits their manufacturers advertise or that have dangerous side effects.

While these government regulations protect consumers from dishonest sellers, regulations are not without cost. The FDA approval process of testing drugs can take years, sometimes preventing potentially life-saving drugs from reaching the market until approval has been granted. Lemon laws prevent individuals who are willing to take a risk on a potentially low-quality car from doing so. Certification of professionals raises barriers to entry by potential competitors and, therefore, may limit the supply of services and result in higher prices. An economic analysis of each of these government regulations and its impact on the market must weigh the benefits provided to consumers of these products, which presumably cannot be provided using existing market mechanisms, against the costs to government and industry of imposing the regulations.

Table 8.1.
Markets with Imperfect Problems and Solutions

Market	Problems	Market Solutions	Government Solutions
Legal Services	Client: quality of lawyer/legal service cannot be easily judged by client Lawyer: guilt/innocence difficult to determine prior to employment	Lawyer's reputation and success, education, partnership in well-known firm, price	State bar exams, legal recourse of suing lawyer
Computer Software	Customer: quality/usefuless of product difficult to judge prior to purchase Seller: once purchased customer has incentive to return product for refund after installation on hard drive	Limited guarantees, reputation of product/company, computer magazine reviews	Consumer product laws
Consumer Credit	After receiving goods/services consumer has incentive to stop payments	Credit reports, requirements of collateral	Regulation of credit and credit reporting markets, criminal law
Insurance Markets	Insuree: incentive to misrepresent driving ability, health, quality of car or house, etc.; incentive to take fewer precautions or less care when driving or maintaining home or health. Insurer: incentive to underfund investments, potential for declaring bankruptcy under large claims	Physicals, home inspections, data on driving record, contractual obligations for fire alarms, health care, etc.; company reputations	Insurance laws and regulating agencies, criminal laws
Labor Markets	Employee: incentive to misrepresent abilities, incentive to 'shirk' while on the job Employer: incentive to misrepresent employee duties, dangers of workplace	Potential employee's education and work history, references, potential employer's reputation, ability to terminate (fire/quit) employment	Regulation of employment contracts, regulation of workplace safety
Stock Market	Incentive for corporate managers to inflate value/profitability of organization, uncertainty about corporate value	Corporate annual reports, investment experts, stock price as a signal of market information on corporate value, diversification of stock portfolio	Enforcement of general accounting principles, criminal law, monitoring by Securities and Exchange Commission
Journal Subscription	Individual subscriber/library cannot determine quality of journal until after paying for and receiving subscription	Journal reputation and age, reputation of editors, citation of published articles, library use	None

Information Markets

Whenever information is bought and sold, there is the potential for the problem of imperfect information, or asymmetrical information, to cause market failure.

Insurance Markets

Insurance markets are, fundamentally, markets of imperfect information. Insurance companies try to determine the potential risk of claims by clients by getting full information from them. When clients apply for life or health insurance, they are asked to have a physical exam and provide a medical history, so that the company can accurately calculate the risk of a medical or life claim. Insurance companies also search driving records, credit records, and require the potential insured to provide detailed information about life-style, gender, employment, and financial assets. All this information is used to determine the potential risk of the insured and to set a fair market premium according to this risk; the higher the risk, the higher the premium.

To lower their premiums, potential clients have a clear incentive to understate their level of risk. This is known as *adverse selection,* which is the problem of high-risk clients misrepresenting their level of risk and paying the premiums of low-risk individuals, thereby preventing market efficiency. High-risk clients may be smokers or have poor driving abilities, poor health, or other attributes that make them a poor insurance risk. If these individuals cannot be distinguished from those with lower risk, their presence in the "pool" of clients increases the number of accidents, deaths, and health problems to a level greater than that of the lower-risk clients. The increase in the level of accidents, deaths, and health risk requires insurance companies to pay out more in claims and, as a result, increases insurance premiums for all clients, low- or high-risk. However, if low-risk individuals have an accurate assessment of their risk, they are unwilling to pay premiums associated with individuals in a higher-risk pool. If premiums rise too much because of adverse selection, low-risk individuals will cancel their insurance policies. Their departure from the pool of clients increases the average level of risk of the pool and necessitates a further increase in premiums. If this trend continues, the problem of adverse selection will result in only high-risk individuals paying high premiums for insurance, while those with low risk are unable to find affordable insurance.

While there are insurance companies willing to supply insurance to low-risk individuals at a reasonable price, the insurance market for low-risk individuals cannot exist if these clients cannot be distinguished from those with higher risk. As in the case of the market for used cars, the market for insurance will not be socially efficient. To correct for the problem of adverse selection, insurance companies check the backgrounds of potential clients to assign them to the correct risk pool. Individuals with good driving records, good health records, or who take classes in defensive driving are identified as being of a lower risk and receive discounted premiums.

A second problem common in insurance markets is *moral hazard,* which occurs when an insured feels that the payout for a claim will be greater than their loss. This belief may encourage an insured to carelessly or recklessly or, worse, to deliberately cause an accident. Insurance companies try to counter moral hazard by putting requirements on insurance policies to prevent careless behavior, by requiring fire detectors in the home, giving discounts for the successful completion of defensive driving classes, and making lower payouts to victims of car accidents who were not wearing their seat belts. Legislation— such as seat belt laws, building codes and inspections, and drunk driving laws—also discourages careless behavior.

Education

Mincer (1974), Spence (1973), and other economists have modeled education as an investment in human capital.[2] Students invest in their human capital by spending time acquiring an education and paying tuition in hopes of receiving a return on their investment in the form of a higher salary or preferred occupation. Education is an investment in building a stock of knowledge to be used in later employment. As an investment, education is a durable good that depreciates. A doctor, lawyer, or librarian acquires a stock of knowledge that will be used for many years of employment. However, as new medical skills, new laws, and new information technologies become available, the old stock of knowledge depreciates, or loses value, requiring individuals to reinvest in new education or new knowledge to maintain their salaries and keep their jobs.

An investment in education also signals an individual's potential performance as an employee. Because employers want to identify capable employees prior to employment, there is a market for information on potential employees. An education or degree is a signal to employers of the ability of a potential employee. A high school graduate may have more ability than someone who did not graduate from high school. A college graduate may have more ability than someone who did not graduate from college. Someone with a doctorate in economics is potentially a better economist than someone with a master's degree. The alma mater's reputation also provides information about the training and ability of the individual. Someone with a medical degree from the University of Chicago may be a better physician than someone with a medical degree from an institution that does not have the same high standards and level of quality.

Other Information Markets

There are several other examples of markets prevented from achieving economic efficiency by imperfect information. These include the markets for religion, marriage, and employment. In the religious market there are several "sellers"—priests, rabbis, sheiks, and ministers. Each seller believes they have the best information about the "true" religion or method of salvation. Unlike used-car dealers, though, suppliers of religious services may be as uninformed as consumers about their religious beliefs. Consumers, with less than perfect information, must decide which is the correct religion. Obviously social efficiency cannot be attained unless everyone chooses the correct religion. However, given the inevitable lack of perfect information, it is not possible for social efficiency to improve in the market of religion.

The same problems of imperfect information occur in the marriage market. Dating and courtship are mechanisms through which people acquire more information about a potential spouse. When a couple feels they have obtained satisfactory information about the spousal potential of each other, the couple marries, in part to prevent the other from continuing to seek information about other potential spouses. Given that information is imperfect, if a wrong choice is made, the result is a divorce. Video dating services, personal advertisements, private investigators, and blood tests are all information services that allow the marriage market to function more efficiently.

Employment and labor markets can also be modeled as markets for information. A prospective employee must provide a resume, references, and information about level of education and previous work experience to a prospective employer. This information is used by the employer to determine efficient matches between prospective employees and available jobs. Employment services and employee "headhunters" collect information from both prospective employees and employers to make efficient matches. Once employed, information may still be collected on the employee to ensure maximum job performance. Measures of productivity, drug testing, and periodic employment reviews are conducted to improve the firm's efficiency by identifying high-quality employees for promotion and low-quality employees for termination.

Modeling Information Acquisition

Information about a potential spouse or worker, about the likely path of a hurricane, or whether a patient needs an operation has value. Acquiring information increases economic efficiency by increasing one's ability to make beneficial decisions. When doctors, lawyers, weather forecasters, or mechanics make decisions based on imperfect information, there is a greater risk that the decision is wrong. The more information a doctor has about a patient's illnesses, the more likely she is to prescribe the correct treatment. Lawyers who are better informed about the law and the case are more likely to make correct decisions, decreasing the time spent in court, their chances of failure, and perhaps even their clients' bills. If weather forecasters have access to the latest satellite imagery, they are better equipped to make accurate weather predictions.

Using our example of medical information for doctors, a simple model can be developed that illustrates the benefits and costs of information acquisition. Assume that when a patient has a specific set of symptoms—high fever, blood in urine, and so on—there is a 50 percent chance that this patient will need an operation and a 50 percent chance that the patient can be cured with a less expensive drug treatment. Assume that the operation costs $100,000 and the drug treatment costs $1,000. Also assume that given the advanced state of the patient's illness, a decision must be made immediately whether or not this patient will receive an operation.

If the risk of making the wrong decision and prescribing medication instead of operating is the death of the patient, then every doctor and patient will choose the operation, even though 50 percent of those operations will not be needed.

While this example might seem extreme, it illustrates the decisions that medical personnel must make every day (to perform a cesarean section or not, to try this antibiotic or another, to operate or wait, to try this drug treatment or an alternative, and so on). In each case different costs are assigned to possible treatments with different chances that a patient with a given set of symptoms may be cured by a given treatment. A doctor weighs the potential benefit his patient will receive based on the chance the treatment will be effective against the effect on the patient if the treatment is unsuccessful. The doctor's decision is based on the patient's symptoms and any tests that can be performed to help identify his illness.

How much is the information about the patient's illness worth? In the previous example, every patient must spend $100,000 for the operation. However, if a test could be developed to determine which patients could be cured with drug treatment, 50 percent of the operations could be avoided, saving $100,000 times the number of avoided operations minus $1,000 for each drug treatment. If 100 operations were performed each year prior to the invention of this test, then the test will save (100 x 0.50) x ($100,000-$1,000) = $4,850,000.

How much is the information worth to a patient? Again, to simplify this example several assumptions must be made. First, assume that the only cost of the operation or the drug is the financial cost. Also assume that patients and doctors use their expected benefit or costs, in a probabilistic sense, as equivalent to the actual benefits or costs. In other words, a 50 percent chance that the operation is needed and costs $100,000 and a 50 percent chance that the drug is needed and cost $1,000 is equivalent to a cost of $50,500 [(0.50 x $100,000) + (0.50 x $1,000) = $50,500]. This means that patients and doctors are *risk neutral.*

Prior to the creation of a test that would identify the patient's illness, the patient was willing to spend $100,000 on the operation. With the test, the patient now knows that there is a 50 percent chance he may need to spend $100,000 on an operation and a 50 percent chance he may need to spend only $1,000 on the drug. On average, the expected expenditure is (0.50 x $100,000 + (0.50 x $1,000) + T, where 'T' is the cost of the test. To be no worse off than he was before, in a probabilistic sense, this expected payment would have to be less than or equal to the $100,000 he would have to pay without the test. Therefore, if T is less than or equal to $49,500, the patient will be no worse off because (0.50 x $100,000) + (0.50 x $1,000) + $49,500 = $100,000. Again, assuming 100 operations per year, patients would be willing to pay $49,500(100)=$4,950,000 per year for this test.

In the more general case, let "p" be the probability of an event such as an operation. Then (1-p) is the probability of that event not occurring. Let "C_p" be the cost of that event and '$C_{(1-p)}$' be the cost of the event not occurring. If "K" is the cost of the action taken without perfect information, then patients are willing to pay as much as "T" for a test as long as

$$pC_p + (1-p)C_{(1-p)} + T < K \qquad (8.1)$$

Rarely does a test or other piece of information tell someone, with certainty, whether an operation or a new carburetor is needed, whether to take their umbrella to work, or whether they are going to win their legal case. Usually the information increases one's knowledge of the chance of events happening rather than the certainty of them happening. In this case, the willingness to pay for the information is the change in the expected value of the result. For example, if access to a legal information database increases the knowledge of an attorney and his ability to be victorious in a case, then the value of that information is the increase in the chance of winning multiplied by whatever the payout might be.

To model this, let "p" be the probability of an attorney winning a legal suit with a value of 'S' if she wins. Then (1-p) is the probability of losing with no payout if she loses. The expected payout from the suit equals the probability the attorney wins multiplied by the payout if she wins plus the probability she loses multiplied by her loss:

$$\text{Expected Payout} = pS + (1-p)0 = pS \qquad (8.2)$$

For example, when similar cases are filed in court by this attorney she may win 50 percent of the cases and receive a portion of the settlement such that her payout or salary is, on average, $1,000,000. This attorney's expected payout from a similar case is $500,000.

Assume that this attorney now has access to a legal librarian and a legal database that can be searched to increase the probability of winning the suit. Let $p^*>p$ be the probability of winning, given that the legal librarian and database are employed for this case at a cost T. The expected payout from the suit then equals:

$$\text{Expected Payout} = p^*S - T \qquad (8.3)$$

As long as the expected payout from winning the case with the help of the legal librarian (equation 8.3) is greater than the expected payout from winning the case without the legal librarian (equation 8.2), then it is worthwhile to employ the librarian and database

$$p^*S - T > pS \qquad (8.4)$$

Rearranging terms, this is equivalent to

$$T < (p^*-p)S \qquad (8.5)$$

In other words, as long as T (the cost of the librarian and database) is less than $(p^*-p)S$ (the difference in the expected payout from winning) it is worth employing the librarian and database. If, for example, the employment of a law librarian and legal database increases the chance of winning a $1,000,000 suit by only 5 percent, the employment has an expected value of $50,000.

The most difficult part about measuring the value of information acquisition is in measuring the parameters of the model—p^*, p, and S. In this example, the law firm could calculate the percentage of cases won with and without the benefit of the law librarian as an estimate of p^* and p, while the average payout in similar cases could be used as an estimate of S. Alternatively, one could measure the willingness-to-pay by attorneys for law librarians, law firms' investments in legal libraries and librarians, or the amount of time lawyers spend or employ others to use legal databases. All of the above would proxy for a lawyer's expected value of access or marginal benefit from this type of information.

Summary

Markets with asymmetric information create a distrust between buyers and sellers that results in the market failing to achieve the socially efficient level of output. To solve this problem, sellers can guarantee product quality, and buyers can acquire additional information about the value of the product. Government regulations may also be used to ensure product quality and safety.

Markets for information suffer, by definition, from problems of asymmetric information, such as moral hazard and adverse selection. However, specific information markets evolve to correct for these problems.

The value of the information acquired depends on its usefulness in assessing the chances of different events occurring and the costs or benefits of these different events. For example, the value of weather information depends on the increased validity of weather forecasts and the costs and benefits incurred from different weather systems. Individual demand or willingness-to-pay for information depends on individual assessment of this information value.

Discussion Questions

1. In 1992, Overs Enterprises in New York State began selling "HIV negative" cards to college students, who wished to reassure potential sexual partners that they did not carry the AIDS virus. The cards gave the results of the student's most recent blood tests, stating that the tests had proven to be HIV negative. The attorney general of the state of New York sued the company for providing false and misleading information. The attorney general's office felt that the cards provided dated information about an individual's HIV status, so that the cards were by their very nature misleading. Comment on this information market. If the cards were allowed for sale, what would happen in the market for sex? Under what conditions would allowing the sale of cards lead to more people getting infected with HIV? How could it lead to fewer people getting infected? Should the attorney general have stopped Overs Enterprises?

2. List three examples, not previously mentioned, where information is sold. How does the level of risk and level of investment influence the availability and price of the information?

3. When ordering books for libraries, bibliographers who specialize in topics are required to have sufficient information about expected use for each title. What information is provided by the name of the author and publisher that would assist the bibliographer in ordering books? How does communication between bibliographers and faculty influence the efficient selection of books and journals?

4. Describe how you would model the value of a medical library to a hospital or the value of a law library to a legal firm. How could you demonstrate whether the hospital or legal firm was spending too much or too little on the library?

Notes

1. George A. Akerlof, "The Market for 'Lemons': Quality Uncertainty and the Market Mechanism," *Quarterly Journal of Economics* 84, no. 3 (1970): 488-500.

2. Jacob Mincer, *Schooling, Experience, and Earnings* (New York: Columbia University Press, 1974); and Michael Spence, "Job Market Signaling," *Quarterly Journal of Economics* 83, no. 3 (1973): 355-74.

Information as a Commodity Versus Information as a Public Good

Information can be modeled both as a commodity and a public good. When buyers and sellers exchange information services or products in markets, information is a private good or commodity. Books sold at a bookstore, newspapers sold on the street corner, computer software for individual use, individual journal subscriptions, and individual phone service are all examples of information goods or services as commodities. In each case, the service or good provides benefit to a single consumer who pays for the supply of that service or good.

Information services or products can also be public goods. Books sold to libraries, newspapers shared by coworkers, computer software networked among several work stations, a library journal subscription, and a telephone network are all examples of information goods or services as public goods. In these examples there are several individuals who benefit from the consumption of the same good. Several patrons can use the same book or journal from the library over the course of a year. Several people can simultaneously use computer software on a network. Everyone uses the same telephone network.

The same good or service can also be modeled both as a public and a private good. The appropriate model depends on the goals of the economic analysis. The public good model examines the collective benefit of a good or service. The decisions of how to finance a good, who should pay for it, and how much each individual should pay will be determined by studying the collective benefit of several individuals. The private good model assumes that a single individual receives the entire benefit from the consumption of a good or service. Production of a private good is usually financed by individual consumers purchasing individual units of the good for their private benefit. The level of output in the market is determined by the demand and supply of the good.

The "commodity" or "private good" model of information goods or services is a model in which individuals benefit from their consumption and expect to pay for the benefits they receive in the same way they purchase other private goods. The "public good" or "social good" model of information goods and services is a model in which there is a collective benefit that consumers or individuals receive from a good or service. The choice of model—public good or commodity—can be illustrated by examining the market for books and journals purchased by individuals and libraries and the market for computer software research and development.[1]

The Market for Books and Journals

The market for books and journals has both private-good and public-good characteristics.[2] The purchase of books and journals by faculty, students, libraries, or other consumers is a private good. Each buyer weighs the benefits that result from their purchase against the cost of the book or journal. In the case of individual consumers, the benefit from purchasing a book or journal is received by the consumer. In the case of a book being purchased for a library, though the library benefit is delivered to many patrons, the purchase is made by a single agent—an acquisitions librarian—who must weigh the benefits to all potential users. As with an individual consumer, the benefits received by library patrons must exceed the book or journal's purchase price. Figure 9.1 illustrates the market for books.

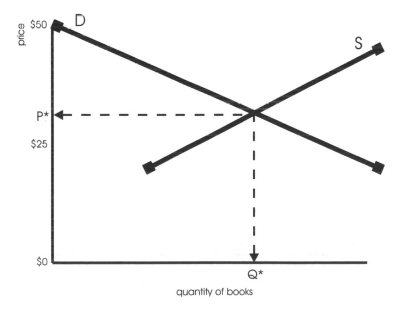

Figure 9.1. The Library's Market for Books.

The demand for books can be divided between library and non-library consumers. Non-library purchases of books include books sold at retail outlets and ordered from publishers. Non-library purchases represent more than 95 percent of the market for books. Libraries represent less than 5 percent of the total market for books, but because of their higher benefits from books, based on the collective benefits of their patrons, library demand is concentrated on the upper range of the market demand curve.

For purposes of this illustration, figure 9.1 assumes that publishers charge each consumer the same price for a book. In addition, this represents the supply of books by all publishers, not just a single publisher. The upward-sloping supply curve (S) means that an increase in the average price of a book will result in publishers offering more books for sale.

Q* is the equilibrium quantity of books sold. If the demand curve (D) in figure 9.1 accurately reflects the marginal benefit from books, then Q* is also the economically efficient or pareto optimum number of books. For individual consumers of books, the demand curve will accurately represent the private marginal benefit or willingness to pay for books. However, it is unclear whether the demand for books by libraries accurately reflects the marginal benefit library patrons receive from books. For the library demand to accurately reflect patron marginal benefits, acquisitions librarians must be able to accurately measure or estimate the value of their library books to patrons. The difficulty of estimating this value to patrons is illustrated in figure 9.2.

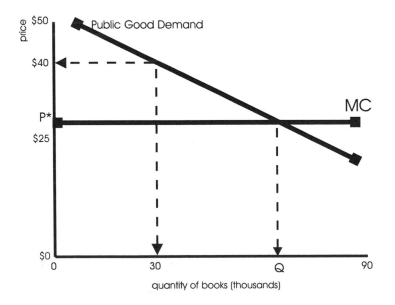

Figure 9.2. The Gotham Public Library's Demand for Books.

Figure 9.2 shows the public-good demand or public-good marginal benefit curve for books in a hypothetical public library. The sum of the marginal benefits of individual patrons who use the library equals the marginal benefit or public-good demand curve for books in the library. In figure 9.2 the 30,000th book purchased by the Gotham Public Library has a marginal benefit of $40. This $40 marginal benefit might represent the use of a book by four patrons, each of whom receives $10 in benefit from that particular book.

The marginal cost (MC) of a book for the library equals the market equilibrium price (P*) in figure 9.1. For simplicity the assumption has been made that the cost of cataloguing the book is trivial. Therefore, the economically efficient number of books purchased by the Gotham Public Library is Q, where the marginal benefit (here called public good demand) of a book equals the marginal cost to the library.

If librarians can accurately predict their patrons' marginal benefit from books, then the actual demand or willingness to pay for books by libraries will reflect the public-good demand or marginal benefit that patrons receive from the libraries. An estimate of the value of books to patrons can come from library patron surveys, user data, and local referendums on public library funding.

It is unlikely that librarians will have full information about their patrons' marginal benefit or that voters in public elections and library patrons are the same group and share common preferences. If, for example, voters underrepresent the marginal benefit library patrons receive from the public library, the library budget approved by voters will be less than the actual marginal benefit of patrons. If the number of books the library purchases at P* is less than Q, the demand for books in figure 9.1 will be less than the marginal benefit of book purchases. The number of books purchased will be less than Q*.

Because marginal benefit has been underrepresented, resulting in lower demand, only Q' books are purchased in figure 9.3, which is less than the economically efficient level of books, Q*. Books between Q' to Q* have a marginal benefit, to library patrons, that is greater than the marginal cost of producing these books, and, as a result, deadweight loss or economic inefficiency is produced. This deadweight loss is represented by the shaded area in figure 9.3.

The demand for books by individual consumers accurately reflects the marginal benefit they receive from books, and the market is able to achieve an economically efficient output. However, with public goods, if the collective financing mechanism does not accurately reflect the marginal benefit to consumers, there will be economic inefficiency. In other words, if voters, acquisitions librarians, library directors, and patrons are unable to translate patrons' marginal benefits into library financing and purchasing policy, there will be economic inefficiency.

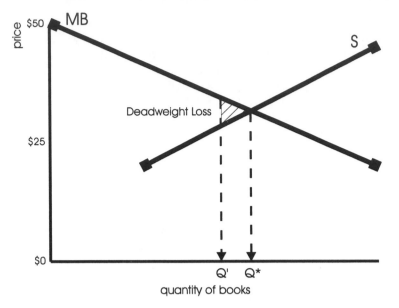

Figure 9.3. The Library's Market for Books when Marginal Benefit Is Underestimated.

As with most public goods, information services and products that require government financing or voluntary contributions may not be efficiently provided. This underscores the need for library directors and voters to gain information about the use and worth of the local library. Patron surveys, voter education, and analysis of library-use patterns are all effective methods of gathering information that can be used to justify financing for the local library.

The Market for Computer Software Research and Development

Not all information goods and services that are public goods rely on government financing. Movies, credit reports, and the news in a newspaper are all public goods financed through sales. A movie is consumed by the people who purchase a ticket to see it. Your credit record is a public good that all potential lenders may access for a fee. The news in a newspaper is read by many individuals simultaneously. Individual subscriptions to the newspaper, as well as advertising revenues pay for the writers, editors, and printers.

The market for computer software also has public- and private-good characteristics. Individuals who purchase copies of the software finance the creativity and innovation required to produce it. The "intellectual property" of the research and development that goes into producing a software program is a public good for all future users of the software.

Figure 9.4 illustrates the market for a hypothetical word-processing program. Given the high fixed costs of developing a software program and the lower marginal cost of producing an additional copy of it, the average cost curve for copies of a program slopes downward. The demand for word-processing programs comes from new academic and business users, users of other word-processing programs, and users of earlier versions of the software.

Manufacturers of computer software can group consumers into several segments and charge a different price to each segment. Usually, business users have a greater demand for the latest version of computer programs; therefore, without an academic affiliation, they must pay a higher price for a copy. Academic users, with more limited resources and lower marginal benefits, pay a lower price than business users. This does not exclude the possibility that some academic users may receive a higher marginal benefit from the software than some business users; it only means that a greater percentage of business users are willing to pay more for the software than academic users. Finally, users of other word-processing programs or of earlier versions have a lower willingness to pay for an upgrade because they can simply continue to use the old program. Therefore, those consumers purchasing upgrades are given a lower price.

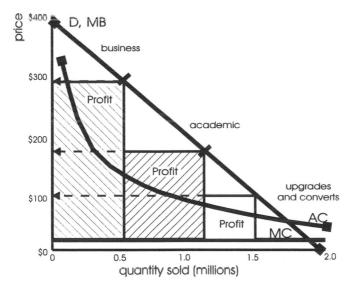

Figure 9.4. The Market Demand for Word-Processing Software.

The inventor of a particular word-processing program maximizes profit by segmenting the market among these three groups of consumers. The copyright on the program, creating a monopoly on that specific intellectual property, enables the inventor to make revenues in excess of marginal costs that can then be used to cover the costs of creative activity or innovation. This profit also motivates software creators and manufacturers to improve their products through additional research and development.

The marginal benefit to software manufacturers of research and development is the sum of the expected profit from individual consumers. In other words, research and development is a public good in that individual marginal benefit from an upgraded computer program is represented by the profit that a software corporation might receive from the sale of that upgrade. Figure 9.5 illustrates this public-good characteristic of research and development.

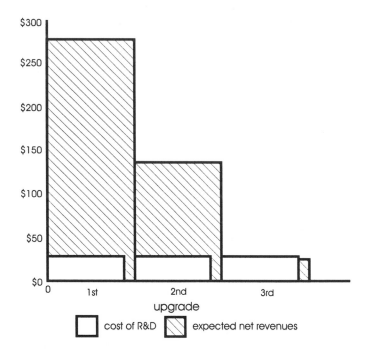

Figure 9.5. The Benefit and Cost of Upgrades.

In figure 9.5, the demand for research and development for the first version of this word-processing program is the sum of the expected profit from each copy sold. As additional versions are invented, fewer users are willing to pay to upgrade their program or switch from other word-processing programs. As a result, each successive upgrade developed has a lower level of profit per unit and a lower expected total profit.

In figure 9.5, the first two upgrades have an expected profit greater than their costs and are, therefore, economically efficient investments. However, the third upgrade does not produce sufficient profit to cover its cost. In a few years, as consumer tastes change, personal computers improve, or more consumers purchase personal computers, the expected profit from additional upgrades may increase and exceed the cost of research and development of the third upgrade.

As the previous example illustrates, modeling information goods or services as public goods does not imply that government financing is the most efficient way to pay for the good. Much research and development is financed using exclusionary user fees. Similarly, modeling an information good or service as a private good does not imply that user fees or prices are the most efficient mechanism for finance. Many information goods and services that might logically be modeled as private goods are efficiently financed through taxes, donations, and advertising. Public library reference services, magazines, and education can be modeled as private goods, yet they are financed in a variety of ways. Reference librarians, paid for by tax revenues and donations, are asked questions by individual patrons who might otherwise be charged user fees for the information received. In this case, the cost of imposing and collecting user fees may outweigh the value of the service, making user fees an inefficient method of financing. Examples of other private goods that are financed in ways other than user fees include magazines, which are financed by sales and advertising revenues, and education, which is financed by tuition, donations, and government funding.

Summary

Information goods and services can be modeled as public or private goods. The choice of model depends on the economic analysis to be done. If the good or service provides a collective benefit to more than one consumer, it should be modeled as a public good. If the good or service provides a private benefit to individual consumers, it should be modeled as a private good or commodity.

In either case, there are several potential methods of financing the good or service. Collective mechanisms such as tax revenues and donations are usually used to finance public goods. However, advertising revenues and exclusionary user fees can also be used to finance public goods. Private information goods and services may also be financed by user fees, advertising revenues, taxes, and donations.

Discussion Questions

1. Consider each of the following information markets: popular movies on video, popular magazines, highway billboards, information on dangerous drugs. How are these products public goods? How are these markets private goods?

2. Discuss the possible methods of financing the markets in the previous question. Comment on the efficiency of the different methods of finance.

Notes

1. For additional insight on the distinction between information as a commodity and information as a public good, see Roger A. McCain, "Information as Property and as a Public Good: Perspectives from the Economic Theory of Property Rights," *The Library Quarterly* 58, no. 3 (July 1988): 265-82; and Yale M. Braunstein, "Information as a Commodity: Public Policy Issues and Recent Research," *Information Services: Economics, Management, and Technology*, eds. R. M. Mason and J. E. Creps (Boulder, CO: Westview Press, 1981), 9-22.

2. For a more technical treatment of the public good–private good characteristics of journals and books, see Janusz A. Ordover and Robert D. Willig, "On the Optimal Provision of Journals qua Sometimes Shared Goods," *American Economic Review* 63, no. 3 (June 1978): 324-38; W. Paul Zahray and Marvin Sirbu, "The Provision of Scholarly Journals by Libraries via Electronic Technologies: An Economic Analysis," *Information Economics and Policy* 4, no. 2 (1989-1990): 127-54; Stanley J. Liebowitz, "The Impact of Reprography on the Copyright System," report for the Bureau of Consumer and Corporate Affairs of Canada, 1981.

Part III

An Introduction to Cost-Benefit Analysis

User Fees

The librarian's creed includes the goal of free flow and open access to information. More often than not this has implied that access to public libraries, government information, and all related services should be free. Charging user fees for access to these services seems to violate the principle of free flow and open access.

Conversely, commercial firms provide little information without a charge or at least the intent of generating sales. The car sales agent may provide you with free information about the automobile you are considering purchasing and about competitors' automobiles, but this information is intended to generate sales. In addition, what the automobile dealer tells you may misrepresent the value of the car or the competitor's car. Similarly, free advertising, while provided free of user fees to the intended audience, is designed to increase sales of specific goods or services.

This difference in attitudes toward the supply of information raises some questions: When should information providers sell information? When should society use market mechanisms such as prices and user fees to finance and restrict access to information? If access to information is sold, what price should be charged? For some time now, user fees for government information and libraries have been the topic of heated professional debate. Braunstein (1979), Van House (1983), Budd (1989), and countless others have contributed research to this debate.[1]

Prices serve a dual purpose: 1) to allocate the supply of goods and services; and 2) to finance the production of these goods and services. Prices as allocation mechanisms determine who can purchase certain goods and services. Only those consumers who receive a benefit from the good greater than the price will purchase it. This ensures that consumers with the most benefit from a good will receive it and that consumers do not abuse or take for granted their consumption of a good. There are many examples of information goods that consumers would abuse if they were free. For example, if the photocopy machines in academic libraries were free people would make copies of their faces, hands, or other body parts to entertain themselves. As a more significant example, the New York State Library does not charge overdue book fines. As a result, because there are no penalties for overdue books, many inconsiderate patrons do not return borrowed books, and the library sends out countless overdue notices. Most libraries charge overdue book fines to avoid this problem.

Prices also serve to finance the production of a good or service. The primary purpose of sales of books, journals, newspapers, software, movies, and any other commercial information product is to pay for costs and generate profits. The purchase price of a computer software program pays for the cost of the floppy disks, for the production of the instruction manual, to compensate authors for their intellectual property, and to compensate the company's owners for their creativity and management skills. Movie tickets, video rental charges, telephone charges, and the price of a newspaper are all user fees collected to finance the production of these goods and services.

Revenues from user fees are also used to finance output in the nonprofit and government sectors. In a library, photocopy revenues are used to purchase paper, toner, and lease the photocopy machine, while overdue book fines can be used to purchase more books. Governments may charge for genealogical records, driver records, or other government documents. These fees finance government expenses including the cost of providing the information.

In the case of information goods and services, a price's allocation role and the financing role frequently conflict. Books, journals, and computer software all have high first-copy costs but relatively low marginal costs for additional copies. The allocative function of user fees requires a price equal to marginal costs to achieve economic efficiency. However, marginal cost pricing with declining average cost curves does not generate sufficient revenue to finance the production of goods or services with high first-copy costs.

This chapter examines the allocative and financing roles of user fees for information goods and services. The first two sections of this chapter examine the allocative function of prices, focusing on setting price to achieve an economically or socially efficient allocation while disregarding the need for revenues. The last section of this chapter examines Ramsey prices, which balance the need for revenues with economic efficiency.

User Fees as Allocation Tools

Whether user fees are charged for photocopying, library information, or government information, prices equal to marginal costs maximize the benefit to consumers or patrons compared to the cost of producing the information. The efficiency of marginal cost pricing is illustrated by figure 10.1, which shows the demand, or marginal benefit and marginal cost, of photocopying in an academic library.

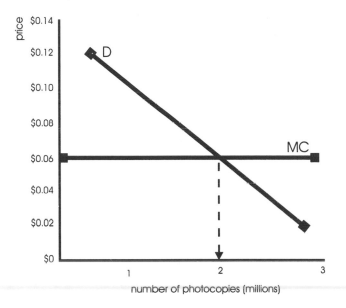

Figure 10.1. Marginal Cost Pricing of Library Photocopying.

In figure 10.1, the marginal cost of a photocopy is $0.06. These are costs associated with the consumer's use of the copier but do not include fixed costs that are incurred regardless of any consumer's level of use. Marginal costs include the cost of paper, toner, and employee time needed for assistance. Fixed costs include the annual leasing or replacement cost of the photocopy machine.

Given the marginal cost, or demand (D), and marginal benefit as illustrated in figure 10.1, the optimal price of a photocopy is $0.06. At that price, the level of output at two million copies is such that the marginal benefit from an additional photocopy equals the marginal cost. If the price were set below $0.06, too many copies would be made because copies would be made at a marginal cost greater than the marginal benefit. If the price were set above $0.06, too few copies would be made because copies could be made at a marginal benefit greater than the marginal cost. At any price other than $0.06, an inefficient number of copies will be made.

Figure 10.2 shows the inefficiency that results if the price of a photocopy were $0.10. At a price of $0.10, only one million photocopies are made because the one-millionth photocopy provides a marginal benefit of $0.10, which is greater than the marginal cost of $0.06 to produce it. In fact, all copies between the one-millionth copy and the two-millionth copy provide benefits to consumers that exceed the additional cost of the copy. A price of $0.10 prevents these additional copies from being made and denies consumers the net benefit from them. The inefficiency or deadweight loss resulting from a price of $0.10 per copy is represented by the shaded area in figure 10.2.

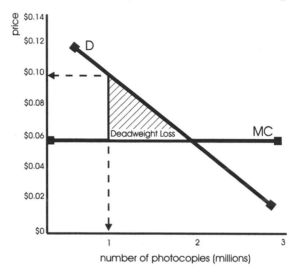

Figure 10.2. Inefficiency in Library Photocopying Because of High Price.

Figure 10.3 illustrates what would happen if the price of a copy were only $0.04. In this case, photocopies would be made that have a marginal benefit less than the marginal cost of producing them. At $0.04 a copy, the two-and-one-half-millionth copy has a marginal benefit of $0.04 to the patron but a marginal cost of paper and toner of $0.06. The copies in excess of two million each have a benefit less than the costs incurred making these copies. By making copies in excess of two million, suppliers must pay more than the benefit of the copies. The inefficiency or deadweight loss in this case is represented by the shaded area in figure 10.3.

Only a price of $0.06 will ensure that all photocopying with a marginal benefit greater than $0.06 will be done, while copying with a marginal benefit of less than $0.06 will not. Therefore, $0.06 is the price that results in economic efficiency in this market.

The $0.06 for a photocopy also covers the marginal costs—paper, toner, and labor—associated with the photocopy machine. This is the financing mechanism of the price. Each copy results in exactly the marginal cost of providing it to the patron. However, with a charge of $0.06, the fixed costs of leasing or purchasing the photocopier will not be covered.

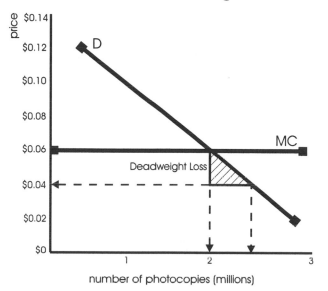

Figure 10.3. Inefficiency in Library Photocopying Because of Low Price.

The Marginal Cost of Pricing

Charging user fees is not cost-free. There is a cost associated with setting prices and collecting revenue. Collecting revenue for photocopying requires the costs of adding Vendacard or coin attachments to the photocopy machine, installing and stocking Vendacard dispensing machines, and collecting the money. Charging user fees requires recording and collecting fees, an activity that, for individual transactions, can add a significant cost to the cost of producing and providing the information.[2]

Because many information products have low marginal cost of production, the cost of pricing may outweigh the benefit of implementing user fees. For example, the marginal cost of borrowing a book from the library is the few seconds that the librarian spends servicing and recording your request. The fixed costs of the book have already been incurred by the library and should not be included in the marginal cost of borrowing. Imposing user fees on patrons equal to the marginal cost of borrowing would generate little revenue and impose the additional costs of collecting fees and maintaining records of this revenue. Not imposing a user fee results in some deadweight loss. Because the book may only be borrowed for a limited time, there will be some patrons who receive a benefit less than the marginal cost of borrowing the book. These patrons will be borrowing in excess of the economically efficient level. However, the costs of imposing user fees would probably be greater than the deadweight loss.

Information sources such as photocopying, reading magazines in a store, database searching, or searching CDs in the library have marginal costs sufficiently low that implementing user fees would not be economically efficient. Figure 10.4 illustrates this using the example of library patrons.

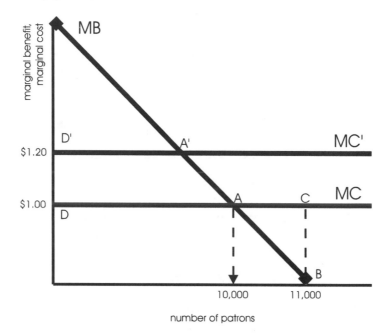

Figure 10.4. Marginal Costs Too Low to Implement User Fees.

Figure 10.4 models the private demand for library services by patrons, the marginal benefit to patrons of using the library, and the marginal cost of servicing these patrons. The marginal cost of servicing a patron is the cost of the time and effort the librarian spends helping the patron and reshelving the returned books. If the librarian spends a total of five minutes on this patron's transaction and is paid $12 per hour, then the marginal cost of a patron's use of the library is $1.

Not charging a user fee invites library use by patrons who have a marginal benefit from library use less than the marginal cost of servicing them. These are the patrons from 10,000 to 11,000 in figure 10.4. The cost of servicing these patrons is the marginal cost ($1) multiplied by the number of extra patrons (1,000). This extra cost equals $1,000. The benefit these patrons receive from using the library is the area under the marginal benefit curve from 10,000 to 11,000. This area equals 0.5 x $1 x 1,000 or $500. The resulting deadweight loss is area ABC, equal to $500 ($1,000 - $500).

To eliminate this deadweight loss, a user fee equal to the marginal cost could be charged to all patrons. However, charging patrons for using the library costs money. Assume each financial transaction costs an additional one minute of the librarian's time. Then the library's costs of charging a fee is $0.20 per patron (1/60th of an hour times $12 per hour). If a user fee is implemented, the new marginal cost of patron use is MC' ($1.20) in figure 10.4—the cost of the patron using the library ($1.00) plus the cost of charging the patron a user fee ($0.20).

Charging patrons a user fee of $1.20 per use of the library will eliminate the deadweight loss of ABC, as patrons who benefit less than $1.20 will no longer use the library. However, this increase in the marginal cost reduces patron-consumer surplus. The reduction in patron-consumer surplus equals area ADD'A'. Area ADD'A' is consumer surplus patrons would have received if there were no user fee, but which they must now give up in the form of a fee to pay for the marginal costs of charging the fee.

If area ADD'A' (the loss of consumer surplus) is greater than area ABC (deadweight loss), implementing user fees is an economically inefficient policy. In figure 10.4, the consumer surplus loss, area ADD'A', is approximately $0.20 x 10,000 patrons, or $2,000. Therefore, patrons and the library will lose more in increased costs or lost consumer surplus ($2,000) than they will gain by eliminating the deadweight loss of patrons who receive less benefit from the library than the cost of servicing them ($500).

The decision of whether or not to charge user fees depends on the elasticity of demand. The less elastic (receptive) patrons are to user fees, the less deadweight loss is eliminated by charging such fees. This is illustrated in figure 10.5.

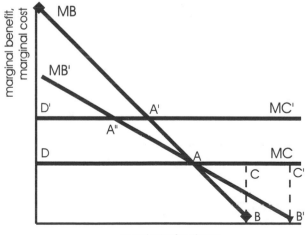

Figure 10.5. Effect of Elasticity of Demand on User Fees.

In figure 10.5, MB' is a more elastic marginal benefit curve than MB. This means that patrons are less likely to use the library if the cost of using it increases. This may be true of small libraries with a limited number of patrons who would object to user fees, libraries near bookstores where patrons are just as willing to purchase books as they are to use the library, or a branch library located in a shopping mall where some patrons might simply be looking for a rest room rather than checking out books.

With a more elastic demand curve for library services, the deadweight loss (area AB'C') resulting from not charging user fees is greater than the deadweight loss (area ABC) with a less elastic curve. This is because the zero price encourages a larger number of patrons who have a marginal benefit of service less than the marginal cost to use the library. In addition, with a less elastic demand curve, the area of potential consumer surplus loss, area ADD'A", is smaller. This implies that it is more likely that economic efficiency will be improved by charging user fees when the demand for information services is elastic.

The efficiency of implementing user fees also depends on the marginal cost of charging. The lower the marginal cost of charging, the lower the loss in consumer surplus from implementing charges. This is illustrated in figure 10.6.

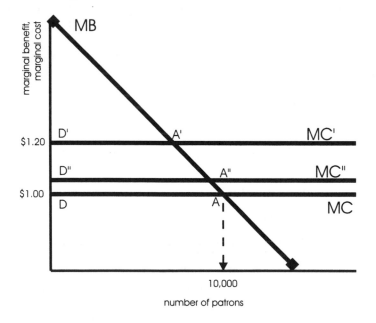

Figure 10.6. Effect of Lower Marginal Costs on Library User Fees.

In figure 10.6, the marginal cost of charging is lowered from $1.20 to $1.01 per patron. This can happen if there is a new electronic system available that makes charging user fees less costly. The lost consumer surplus from charging decreases from area ADD'A' to area ADD"A", or from approximately $2,000 to $100. In this case, because the marginal cost of charging patrons ($100) is less than the deadweight loss from not charging ($500) user fees improve economic efficiency by $400.

Technological advances frequently result in a lower cost of charging fees. New cash registers and bar coding decrease the cost of charging in grocery stores, while improvements in scanning technology have decreased the cost of charging drivers on toll roads. As these technological advances have decreased the costs of charging, they have also decreased the consumer surplus lost when user fees are implemented. As a result, technological advances have increased the chance that implementing user fees for information goods and services might improve economic efficiency.

Ramsey Prices

User fees and prices for information services serve not only to allocate resources but also to finance goods and services. Revenues collected from photocopiers go toward purchasing photocopier supplies; overdue book fees are used to finance library operations; and movie admissions charges finance the movie production and theater operations. The revenues collected from user fees may or may not cover the cost of the service. When costs exceed revenues from user fees, financing from the sale of other goods, taxes, or donations must also be used to cover costs. When revenues exceed costs, there is a profit that, at commercial firms, is used to reward employees, managers, or owners. In the public and nonprofit sectors, excess revenues are used to reward employees or finance other goods.

Library directors and government administrators must determine what prices to charge for services, not only to efficiently supply individual goods and services, but also to finance the production of those goods and services for which sufficient revenues are not collected. For example, it may be worthwhile for the library director to charge a price for photocopying above the marginal cost, and use those surplus revenues to finance the purchase of more books, journals, or other worthy expenditures. Some nonprofit organizations sell magazines and other goods at a profit and use these revenues to finance other services. Universities use surplus tuition revenues to finance computer services for which students and faculty are not charged. In each example, an organization has the ability to price above cost when selling one good and use these surplus revenues to cross-subsidize the production of another good or service, which, for various reasons, cannot cover its own cost but should be provided. How optimal prices are chosen under these circumstances is illustrated in figure 10.7.

Figure 10.7 represents the market for photocopying in a library. Assume that the cost of implementing user fees is minimal so that consideration of the increase in marginal cost is not necessary. This is a reasonable assumption if there is an existing fee for photocopying; simply increasing the amount of this fee will have little effect on the cost of collecting the additional revenues. According to figure 10.7, the economically efficient price to charge for photocopying is $0.08 per copy, an output level at which 2.2 million copies would be made. If a price of $0.09 per copy were charged, there would be a decrease in photocopying to two million copies and a deadweight loss of area ABC equal to $1,000.

While this pricing policy produces a deadweight loss, it also yields revenues above marginal cost. Revenues net of marginal costs equal the difference between $0.09 and $0.08 multiplied by the number of photocopies made, two million. Net revenues equal $20,000, area BCDE. In total, patrons lose $21,000 (ABC + BCDE) in consumer surplus from the price increase.

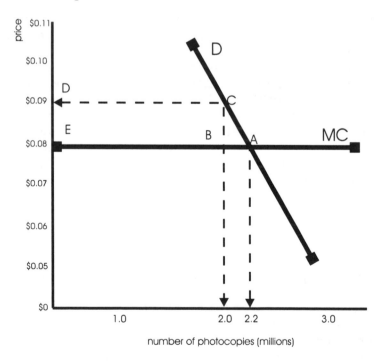

Figure 10.7. Pricing of Library Photocopying to Generate Surplus Revenue.

Economic efficiency depends on the value of the use of this additional revenue. Revenues could go toward hiring an additional reference worker, buying additional books or journals, or paying for capital improvements or for other fixed costs at the library. If these revenues go to hiring an additional reference worker in the library, the net marginal benefit of this worker may be greater than the deadweight loss created by the higher photocopy price. Figure 10.8 shows the marginal benefit and marginal cost of reference workers at this library. If the library budget presently only allows for the employment of two reference workers, but an additional reference worker provides an annual marginal benefit of $30,000 at a cost of $20,000, then library patrons will receive a net marginal benefit of $10,000 from the third reference worker. Library patrons will actually be better off if the price of photocopying is increased to pay for the additional reference worker. Patrons lose $21,000 in consumer surplus but gain $30,000 in benefit from the additional reference worker. In other words, library patrons "purchase" $10,000 in net benefits from the additional reference worker at a cost of $1,000 in deadweight loss from their photocopying. Patrons gain $9,000 net benefit after the price of photocopying is increased to pay for an additional reference worker.

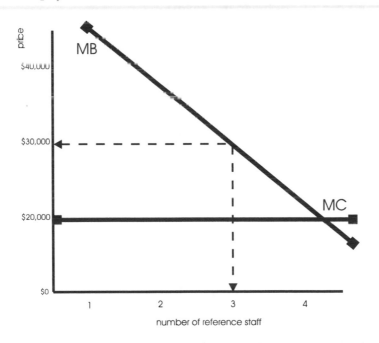

Figure 10.8. Costs and Benefits of Additional Library Reference Staff.

Ramsey prices are a set of optimal prices above marginal cost that provide financing to supply goods and services.[3] Prices above marginal cost that produce deadweight loss in one market are used to finance the production of other goods and services that have a benefit in excess of the deadweight loss. The deadweight loss resulting from increasing the price of photocopying, overdue book fines, or user fees for acquiring government information must be compared to the value of the services purchased with surplus revenues. Economic efficiency is increased when the deadweight loss of increasing the price on one good or service is less than the net benefit produced from the use of the additional revenue. A more detailed analysis of Ramsey pricing in this example is demonstrated in appendix C, on page 177.[4]

An alternative to using library photocopy revenues or imposing government fees is to increase taxes. Unfortunately, increasing taxes on personal income, sales, corporate income, or other sources results in deadweight loss. The best estimate of the deadweight loss from taxing labor income shows $3 in deadweight loss for every $10 in tax revenue.[5] This suggests that prices above marginal cost for many services and goods provided by libraries and government organizations might provide needed revenues at a level of deadweight loss below the level produced through general taxation.

Summary

The allocation role of prices requires that prices be set equal to marginal costs to achieve economic efficiency. Prices above or below marginal costs will result in deadweight loss. If prices are less than marginal costs, some units are consumed at a cost higher than the benefit consumers receive from them. If prices are greater than marginal costs, units that have benefits greater than their costs are not purchased.

A more complete analysis of user fees in information markets must also include the marginal cost of implementing prices and the potential use of surplus revenues. The cost of pricing may imply that implementing user fees for some information goods and services imposes a greater cost on consumers than the decrease in deadweight loss from not charging user fees. However, prices above marginal cost may result in a more efficient level of overall service if the value of services provided with the excess revenues exceeds the deadweight loss incurred. User-fee financing requires a complete analysis of all related goods and services to determine the optimal user fee for any given good or service.

Discussion Questions

1. Show how when the marginal cost of a good or service is increasing, setting price equal to marginal cost may result in excess revenues.

2. Chapter 5 showed that if a good or service has a positive externality, a price less than marginal cost will achieve economic efficiency. How does the presence of a positive or negative externality influence the efficiency of user fees when there is a cost to implement these fees?

3. Library patrons must pay for photocopying and renting conference rooms. Assume that the marginal cost of photocopying is $0.06 per copy and the marginal cost of cleaning a conference room is $10 per use. How does the elasticity of demand for these services influence deadweight loss if a price above marginal cost is charged? Illustrate and explain this. Assume prices above marginal cost must be charged for each service to raise revenues for the library. If you had to choose an optimal set of prices above marginal cost for these two services, how does the elasticity of demand influence the prices you would charge?

Notes

1. Yale M. Braunstein, "Costs and Benefits of Library Information: The User Point of View." *Library Trends* 28, no. 1 (Summer 1979): 79-87; Nancy A. Van House, *Public Library User Fees: The Use and Finance of Public Libraries* (Westport, CT: Greenwood Press, 1983); and John M. Budd, "It's Not the Principle, It's the Money of the Thing," *Journal of Academic Librarianship* 15, no. 4 (1989): 218-22.

2. For an example of the additional costs from collecting user fees from the telephone directory assistance market, see George Daly and Thomas Mayor, "Estimating the Value of a Missing Market: The Economics of Directory Assistance," *Journal of Law and Economics* 23, no. 1 (1980): 147-66.

3. Frank P. Ramsey, "A Contribution to the Theory of Taxation," *Economic Journal* 37 (1927): 47-61.

4. Also see Bruce R. Kingma, "The Demand for Photocopies and Journal Subscriptions: An Empirical Test of the Librarians' Solution to Journal Pricing," unpublished manuscript, School of Information Science and Policy, State University of New York at Albany, 1994; and Bruce R. Kingma and Philip B. Eppard, "Journal Price Escalation and

the Market for Information: The Librarians' Solution," *College & Research Libraries* 53 (November 1992): 523-35.

5. D. W. Jorgenson and K. Yun, "The Excess Burden of Taxation in the U.S.," Harvard Institute for Economic Research, Discussion Paper 1528, 1990.

The Value of Time

11

Many information goods and services require time to consume. Going to a movie, reading a book, attending a lecture, or making a telephone call are all activities that require an investment of time. The price or financial cost of these goods is only a small part of the full economic cost or opportunity cost of consuming them; the value of the time investment is also a cost that needs to be considered. The *opportunity cost* of these goods is the purchase price or fee plus the value of time spent consuming them. The opportunity cost of a movie is the ticket price plus the value of the time spent traveling to and watching the movie. The opportunity cost of a book is the price of the book plus the value of the time spent reading it.

Demand or cost-benefit analysis of these markets must include the value of time spent on consumption to accurately reflect the value of these goods and the willingness of patrons, users, or consumers to pay for them. Using only the financial price paid for these goods or services undervalues both the benefit consumers receive from them and the cost consumers incur. Whenever commercial firms analyze the demand for time-intensive goods and services, the consumers' value of the time spent acquiring these goods is an important factor in the analysis. For example, a three-hour movie epic may be of sufficient quality to sell more movie tickets, however, film studios consider the patron's willingness to spend time to view the movie. Shorter films require less viewing time than three-hour epics. Demand analysis of books, direct marketing, and television ads all include a valuation of consumer time. The optimal length of new books, amount of information sent through direct marketing, or length of a television ad are all influenced by the value of time of potential consumers.

Measuring the value of time is also important in cost-benefit analyses of information goods and services provided by government and nonprofit organizations. Analyses of the benefit and cost of providing books and journals, tax forms, and computer systems require

139

an assessment of the value of time spent using these goods. The opportunity cost of books and journals in a library must include the value of the time spent by patrons reading them. However, there may also be the economic benefit of time saved by patrons, who can get information immediately from the library rather than waiting for a book or journal article to be delivered to them. The opportunity cost of a tax form involves the government's printing and shipping costs as well as the value of time spent by taxpayers filling out the forms. Finally, the opportunity cost of computing systems depends on the processing speed of each system and the value of the employee's time.

New technology may decrease the amount of time spent using information goods or services. For example, a personal computer with a 586 processor is faster than one with a 486 processor. When making a decision to purchase the faster computer, one must consider not only the financial difference between the two computers but also the value of the time it takes to run software using the two different processors. Most libraries now have electronic catalogs to speed patron searching of the library's holdings, a significant time savings compared to the old card catalogs. Libraries also give patrons access to information on compact disks, speeding up the research process compared to comparable print resources.

Failure to include the value of time to users in a cost-benefit analysis can result in serious mistakes in the valuation of particular information systems or services. For example, libraries frequently attempt to save money by canceling underused journal subscriptions and providing them to patrons through interlibrary loan. However, a complete cost analysis of these alternative methods of access must include the value of the time spent by patrons waiting for the articles to be delivered through interlibrary loan.

Measuring the Value of Time

The value of time spent on one activity is the value or cost of foregone opportunities during that time. For example, if you get paid $8.50 per hour and decide to take the last three hours of the afternoon off from work and go to the movies, you will have foregone $25.50 in potential earnings.

The most basic and most frequently used method of measuring the value of time is to use an individual's hourly wage. An attorney may charge clients $150 per hour. If she chooses to spend an hour at lunch instead of an hour at the office with a client, she loses $150. If you make $20 per hour as an academic librarian and choose to "spend" an hour of your time reading a book, the value of the time can be estimated as $20. And if you work as a cashier and make $6 per hour and choose to spend an hour shopping, you are foregoing $6 in wages.

Time spent away from work during the evenings and weekends may also be valued at an individual's wage rate. While not everyone can simply choose to work an extra hour and make an extra $6 or $150, many employees can work additional hours during evenings and weekends. Some employees may work extra hours to increase their job skills or employer's opinion of them, thereby hoping to be promoted and increase their salary. In any case, using an individual's wage rate is a good approximation of the value of an hour to the employee and an approximation of his hourly value to his employer.

Measuring Opportunity Costs

If an individual's hourly wage is used as the value of an hour of their time, the opportunity cost of a good is the price of the good plus the cost of the time, which is the amount of time spent consuming the good times the consumer's hourly wage. Let P be the price of a good, t the time spent consuming it, and w the individual's wage rate; the opportunity cost equals P + tw. For example, if a movie ticket costs $7.50 and the movie lasts 2.5 hours, the opportunity cost of the movie to someone who makes $10 per hour is $32.50 [$7.50 + (2.5 hours x $10 per hour)], while the opportunity cost of the same movie to someone who makes $20 per hour is $57.50 [$7.50 + (2.5 hours x $20 per hour)].

Table 11.1 shows the opportunity cost of other information goods and services, assuming that the consumer's wage rate is $20 per hour.

Table 11.1.
Economic Cost of Time Intensive Goods

	(1) Financial Cost	(2) Time (Hours)	(3) Time Cost (Wage=$20)	(4) Opportunity Cost (1+3)
Movie	$ 7.50	2.5	$ 50.00	$ 57.50
Book	$ 20.00	10.0	$ 200.00	$ 220.00
Long-distance telephone call	$ 6.00	0.5	$ 10.00	$ 16.00
CD search	$ 0.00	0.3	$ 6.00	$ 6.00
"Browsing" library journals	$ 0.00	1.0	$ 20.00	$ 20.00
College class	$900.00	100.0	$2,000.00	$2,900.00

As the wage or the time required to consume the good increases, the opportunity cost increases. A three-hour movie has a greater opportunity cost than a two-hour movie. A 30-minute telephone call has a greater opportunity cost than a 10-minute telephone call. In both cases, if consumers choose to watch the longer movie or make the longer telephone call, it is because they receive more benefit from these goods, even though they have a greater opportunity cost.

Because the opportunity cost of a good depends on an individual's wage, it is individual-specific. Someone with a higher wage has a higher cost of time. This has been shown several times, most recently in a study of sleep by Biddle and Hamermesh (1990).[1] Biddle and Hamermesh showed that individuals with higher wage rates sleep less than those with lower wage rates. It simply costs more for someone with a higher wage rate to sleep. Individuals with higher wages also spend less time shopping, eating, and watching television.

The Value of Time Saved

Many information services save time. The value of the time saved is the benefit consumers receive from these services. For example, can the value of good service to a library patron be measured? Assume the library can employ one of two reference librarians. Assume both librarians are capable of finding the correct answers to patron questions, but one takes an average of five minutes to answer a question while the other librarian takes an average of 10 minutes. The more efficient librarian may be more experienced than the less efficient librarian and may expect a higher salary commensurate with the additional years of experience.

The value of the first librarian to a patron is the five minutes of time saved times the hourly wage of the patron. If the patron makes $20 per hour, then the more efficient reference librarian saves the patron $1.67 (5 minutes x $20/60 minutes) for each question answered. Conversely, the less efficient librarian has an added cost of $1.67 per patron. If these librarians answer an average of 30 reference questions per day over 250 working days a year, the "better" reference librarian saves patrons $12,500 (30 x 250 x 5 x $20/60 minutes) in time per year. Therefore, while the library may save money by hiring a less experienced librarian for a lower salary, the opportunity cost to patrons is higher.

Malcolm Getz (1987, 1988) shows an excellent application of the opportunity cost of time in library services.[2] Getz measured the value of time saved by library patrons using an electronic library catalog versus a card catalog. Study participants were asked to search for a book in the library's collection using the electronic catalogue and the library's card catalog. Getz found that patrons using the electronic catalog could locate library books, on average, 78.5 seconds faster than they could using the card catalog. Given the number of searches per year and the average wage of library patrons, he estimated that the electronic card catalog saved patrons $115,340 worth of time per year.

The value of an hour spent on a good or service is not always equal to the wage an individual earns. The opportunity cost of an hour can be approximated by individuals' wages only when they cannot spend their time in more than one activity. For example, time spent on a bus can be used to read a newspaper, time spent listening to the radio can also be used to fix your car or clean your house, and time spent waiting for a letter or fax can be used to do other activities. In each example, the value of time used in consuming one good cannot be accurately measured by the individual's wage because he or she might be doing more than one thing.

For example, consider the patron's cost of using interlibrary loan. If there is no fee to the patron for requesting a journal article from interlibrary loan, the opportunity cost is the value of the time spent waiting for the article to be delivered; in this case, three days. However, one cannot consider the opportunity cost of these three days as the hourly wage multiplied by the hours waiting because during this time the patron can be performing other activities: studying, doing research, or reading other articles.

There are two ways to measure the value of time spent waiting. First, consumers or patrons can be interviewed about the cost of their time spent waiting for an article to be delivered, or waiting on the bus, or waiting to receive a letter. Unfortunately, as individuals rarely consider the value of time spent waiting, their answers may not be accurate. An alternative is to collect data on the use of or demand for nearly identical goods or services that have different prices and different time costs. The train and bus are both popular with commuters but they have different fares and take different amounts of time to get commuters to their offices. Letters sent first class and through overnight delivery service have different prices and take different amounts of time to deliver. If time is important, individuals may be willing to pay for overnight delivery. These individuals weigh the value of their time spent waiting against their demand curve for overnight delivery.

To further illustrate, assume patrons of interlibrary loan have two alternative methods of document delivery: service A and service B. Service A is free, but takes eight days, on average, to deliver the article. Service B, a commercial delivery service, provides a journal article in two days but charges the patron $11 for delivery. If the patron is given a choice and requests the article from the commercial delivery service, the patron is revealing that the value of the extra six days waiting for the article to be delivered is at least $11.

This type of information can be used by interlibrary loan librarians to determine the benefit of faster delivery to interlibrary loan patrons. While the financial cost, to the patron or the library, may be greater with one type of service, the benefit of the time saved by the patron may exceed this extra financial cost, making it economically efficient to use the faster service. Unfortunately, because patrons are not charged for interlibrary loan services at most academic libraries, the extra benefit provided to patrons from faster service does not result in additional revenues for the library to cover the added costs.

The benefit library patrons receive from a new electronic library catalog, an additional reference librarian, a new computer, or any other improvement in service is the value of time saved. This benefit can then be compared to the cost of the good or service. While it may cost less to hire an inexperienced reference librarian than an experienced one, or purchase a computer with a 486 processor instead of a 586 processor, or use one method of interlibrary loan service versus another, it is the value of time saved to patrons, users, or employees that determines which alternative is more economically efficient.

Consumer Surplus and Economic Cost

In each of the previous examples—reference librarians, computer speeds, and interlibrary loan services—the difference in the opportunity cost measures the value of the time saved by consumers or patrons. However, this underestimates the full value to consumers of a decrease in the economic price of a good or service. If the opportunity cost decreases, the quantity consumers demand will increase. Consumers receive benefit from the decrease in the price plus benefit from the increase in the quantity consumed. The full value to consumers of a decrease in price is the increase in consumer surplus. This is illustrated in figure 11.1.

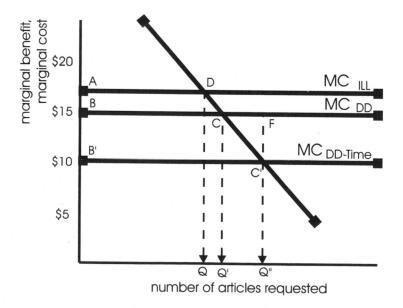

Figure 11.1. Comparative Values of Document Delivery Services.

Figure 11.1 shows the demand or marginal benefit from document delivery or interlibrary loan services for library patrons. Assume that a journal article "costs" the average library patron eight days of waiting at a value of $2 per day, for a "price" of $16. This marginal cost of a journal article delivered by interlibrary loan is represented by MC_{ILL}. Now assume that using a commercial document delivery service takes only five days but charges $5 for each article delivered. If an assumption is made that patrons pay the $5 document delivery charge, they will see a net decrease in the economic cost of delivery from $16 to $15 (the $5 charge plus five days at $2 per day). The marginal cost of commercial document delivery is represented by MC_{DD}. Because patrons pay the commercial delivery fee, there is no difference between the opportunity cost of time spent waiting for delivery and the financial cost of the service. The two costs are summed to determine the economic cost of delivery. The resulting gain in consumer surplus is area ABCD. This consumer surplus gain includes the $1 decrease in marginal cost on the original number of articles requested plus the consumer surplus of the increase in requests (which went from amount D to amount C).

If the library were to pay the $5 fee, instead of the patron, the patron's cost of delivery decreases to $10. This is represented by $MC_{DD\text{-}time}$ in figure 11.1. Unfortunately, if the patron does not pay the document delivery charge, then patrons who receive a benefit from an article less than the full economic cost of $15 will request articles, moving the amount consumed from C to C'. Therefore, a price decrease from $15 to $10 results in an increase in patron consumer surplus of area BB'C'C. The financial cost to the library of the $5 commercial document delivery fee is area B'C'FB. Because the consumer surplus gain to patrons is less than the financial cost of commercial delivery to the library, there is a deadweight loss of area C'CF.

Congestion

Time saved by one person is sometimes saved by others. Time wasted by one person is sometimes lost by others. Time spent can have positive or negative externalities on other consumers. For example, when a new motorist enters a crowded highway he not only increases his own commuting time but slows down all other drivers by increasing congestion. Unfortunately, the new driver never considers the external cost of congestion he imposes on others. The external costs of congestion can be the result of a slow searcher using the CD-ROMs at the library, an employee using the office printer while others are waiting, or a patron who fails to return a book to the library when other patrons want it. As the number of electronic packets sent on the Internet increases, the congestion slows response time for all users.

Information goods and services are sometimes subject to congestion because, as public goods, they are frequently shared by several
users or patrons. The Internet, a computer network, a book in the
library, a computer workstation, and the library reference desk can all
become congested when too many users or patrons try to consume the
same service at the same time. With a limited number of consumers
the service may be non-rival; however, as the number of consumers
exceeds capacity, the service becomes congested. This congestion
imposes a negative externality on users or patrons who must wait to
use a computer terminal or the Internet, read the library book, or ask
a question. The external cost of the congestion on the Internet is
illustrated in figure 11.2.

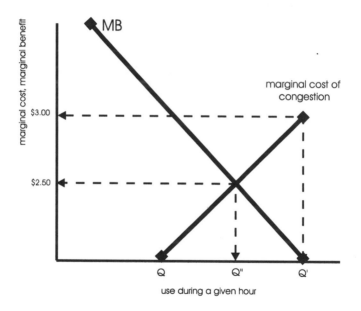

Figure 11.2. External Cost of Congestion on the Internet.

Figure 11.2 illustrates the marginal benefit and external cost of
using the Internet during one typical hour. The marginal benefit curve
in figure 11.2 is the benefit to individual users minus the opportunity
cost of time spent using the Internet during this hour and represents
the private benefit to individuals of their use. With fewer than Q users,
at which point there is economic efficiency, the Internet is a non-rival
good and the marginal cost of any individual using it is zero. However,
when there are more than Q users, there is an external cost of
congestion as traffic and access to the Internet slows.

To calculate the cost of congestion assume that after Q users, each
additional user slows down the flow of traffic by 0.01 seconds each

hour. While this slowdown is minor for any individual user, if Q equals 60,000 users, then, in total, 600 seconds or 10 minutes are lost to the slowdown. If the average wage of a typical Internet user is $12 per hour, then the external cost of an additional user is $2. Initially this cost is minor, but as the number of users increases, congestion increases, and the external costs increase.

Additional users of the Internet do not perceive the cost they impose on other users. Each user only perceives the marginal benefit of his or her individual use and will access the Internet as long as the individual marginal benefit is greater than zero. In figure 11.2, additional users will continue to access the Internet until there are a total of Q' users. If Q' equals 90,000 users, each additional user imposes an external marginal cost equal to $3 (0.01 seconds/user x 90,000 users x $12/hour x 1 hour/3600 seconds). At 90,000 users, the information requests of each user are slowed down by five minutes each hour—30,000 extra users times 0.01 slowdown per extra user—thereby requiring the 90,000 users to "spend" an extra five minutes each to acquire information that, during an uncongested period, would take an hour.

The socially efficient level of Internet use in figure 11.2 is Q" users, where the marginal cost of an additional user equals the marginal benefit that user receives from the Internet. For example, if Q" is the 75,000th user, then the marginal external cost imposed by this user is $2.50, as is the marginal benefit that additional user receives from one hour of access. While the 75,000th user imposes a cost on others, he also receives a benefit greater than this cost and therefore should be allowed to access the Internet. Additional users will impose costs of congestion greater than the marginal benefit they would receive from access.

To achieve the socially efficient level of use, only Q" users should be allowed on the Internet in a given hour. The easiest way to ensure this level of use is to charge users a fee of $2.50 for one hour of access. In this case, only users with a marginal benefit of access greater than or equal to $2.50 will be willing to pay the access fee. Users between Q" and Q' receive less than $2.50 in benefit from access, so they will not be willing to pay the external costs their access would impose on other users.

While charging fees for use of the Internet may be an unpopular idea among users, fees to reduce congestion will actually increase access time to information. Varian and Mackie-Mason (1993) present more complex schemes for Internet pricing.[3]

Present Value

The value of goods also depends on the timing of future costs and benefits. When you purchase a durable good, you expect to receive a benefit from the good over a period of several years. For example, when you purchase a videotape, your willingness to pay for it is not the value of a single viewing. Rather, your benefit from that videotape is the sum of the value you expect to receive from all future viewing. Books, videotapes, computer hardware and software, journal subscriptions, and many other information goods and services are durable goods. In each case, the cumulative value of all future uses of a good determines the demand for that good.

Benefits and costs of durable goods should be measured over time. For example, when a photocopy machine is purchased, there are annual benefits you expect to receive from using the machine, and annual costs of maintenance, supplies, and depreciation. To determine whether it is worthwhile to purchase a photocopy machine, the lifetime stream of future costs and the purchase price should be compared to the stream of future benefits.

But future costs and benefits are not equal to present costs and benefits. They are not worth as much. To illustrate this, assume that you can buy and receive a computer for $1,000 and have a choice of paying the $1,000 today versus paying $1,000 one year from now with no interest. If given a choice, most people would choose to pay the $1,000 a year from now. This is because if you found a bank that paid 5 percent on a risk-free savings account, you could place $952.38 in the bank today and receive $1,000 [$1,000 = $952.38 (1+ 0.05)] one year from now. The value today of $1,000 a year from now at an interest rate of 5 percent is $952.38 [$952.38 = $1,000/(1+ 0.05)]. More generally, if r is the interest rate, C dollars one year from now is worth $C/(1+r)$ dollars today. C dollars two years from now is worth $C/(1+r)(1+r) = C/(1+r)^2$ today because this is the amount of money you would have to put in a risk-free savings account to have C dollars in two years.

The *present value* of C dollars, t years from now at an interest rate of r, is defined as $C/(1+r)^t$. The present value of a stream of dollars C_0, C_1, C_2, . . ., C_n, where subscripts refer to the year in which the dollars are received, equals

$$PV = C_0 + C_1/(1+r) + C_2/(1+r)^2 \ldots + C_n/(1+r)^n \qquad (11.1)$$

If a good or service has a stream of annual costs of $(C_0, C_1, C_2, \ldots, C_n)$ and a stream of annual benefits of $(B_0, B_1, B_2, \ldots, B_n)$ then the *net present value* of it equals:

$$NPV=(B_0-C_0)+(B_1-C_1)/(1+r)+(B_2-C_2)/(1+r)^2 \ldots +(B_n-C_n)/(1+r)^n \quad (11.2)$$

Table 11.2 illustrates the net present value for the purchase of a videotape based on different interest rates, r. Table 11.2 assumes that you use the tape twice in year zero (the first year of ownership), twice in year one, once in year two, but don't use it thereafter. Table 11.2 also assumes that the value of the first use is $10, because the video is new, and the value of each subsequent use is $3.

Table 11.2.
Net Present Value of a Videotape Purchase.

				Net Present Value		
Year	Uses	Benefit	Cost	r=0%	r=5%	r=10%
0	2	$13	($20)	($7.00)	($7.00)	($7.00)
1	2	$6	($0)	$6.00	$5.71	$5.45
2	1	$3	($0)	$3.00	$2.72	$2.48
3	0	$0	($0)	$0.00	$0.00	$0.00
Total Net Present Value				$2.00	$1.43	$0.93
Note: Parentheses indicate negative numbers.						

When the interest rate is zero, the net present value equals the sum of all costs and benefits. However, as the interest rate increases, the value of future benefits decreases while present costs are unchanged, causing the net present value to decrease.

Individual demand for durable goods is based on the net present value a consumer expects to receive from the good. The demand for durable information goods and services by organizations requires managers to determine the present value of benefits and costs for all potential users or patrons. For example, consider the purchase of a photocopy machine by the university library. The net present value is illustrated in table 11.3 and figure 11.3.

Table 11.3.
Net Present Value of a Photocopier.

(1) Year	(2) Use	(3) Revenue	(4) Consumer Surplus	(5) Cost	(6) Net Financial Benefit (3-5)	(7) Net Economic Benefit (3+4-5)	(8) 1/ (1.05)†	(9) Net Present Financial Value (6*8)	(10) Net Present Economic Value (7*8)
0	100,000	$10,000	$6,000	$25,000	($15,000)	($9,000)	1	($15,000)	($9,000)
1	100,000	$10,000	$6,000	$10,000	$0	$6,000	0.9524	0	$5,714
2	100,000	$10,000	$6,000	$10,000	$0	$6,000	0.9070	0	$5,442
3	100,000	$10,000	$6,000	$10,000	$0	$6,000	0.8638	0	$5,183
						Total Net Present Value		($15,000)	$7,339
†Note: Parentheses indicate negative numbers.									

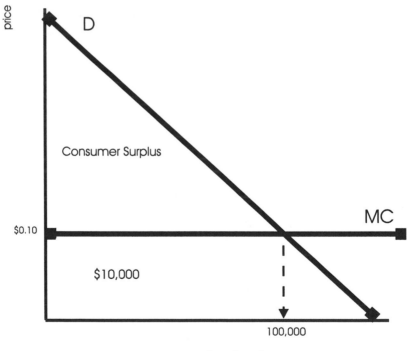

Figure 11.3. Annual Benefit and Cost of Photocopies.

Table 11.3 assumes that the library is considering purchasing a photocopier that will last four years at an interest rate of 5 percent. Future benefits and costs are discounted by the discount factor in column 8. The level of use shown in column 2 and consumer surplus in column 4 can be estimated from data on existing photocopy demand at the library. Table 11.3 assumes that the cost of the photocopier is $15,000 and has an additional $10,000 in annual marginal costs based on an estimated 100,000 uses per year.

If photocopying is priced at the marginal cost of a copy, $0.10, then annual revenue of $10,000 will equal the marginal cost of the photocopier but will not cover the fixed cost of purchasing it. Column 9 in table 11.3 shows that the net present financial value of the photocopier is negative $15,000.

However, the economic benefit of photocopying includes the consumer surplus that users receive from it. According to figure 11.3 and table 11.3, consumers receive $16,000 in benefit from photocopying for which they pay $10,000. The annual consumer surplus from photocopying is $6,000. The net economic benefit is the sum of the revenue and the consumer surplus that users receive from photocopying minus the cost of the copier, shown in column 7. If price is set equal to the marginal cost of a copy, it is economically efficient to purchase the photocopier as long as the consumer surplus exceeds the initial $15,000 cost of the machine. Given the discount factor in column 8, the net present economic value of the photocopier is shown in column 10. According to table 11.3, the net present economic value of the photocopier is $7,339.

While consumer surplus provides benefits to patrons, it does not provide revenue to the library. This means that in this example the library must find alternative sources of revenues (university support, tax support, tuition). The alternative is to increase the price of photocopying to raise the revenue for the purchase of the machine. While this may be necessary to finance the copier, it will produce deadweight loss for this service. Ramsey pricing of photocopying and other services will bring the library as close to its efficient level of service as possible.

Summary

The value of time spent consuming goods and services, waiting for goods or services to be delivered, or waiting for future benefits and costs is an important factor in cost-benefit analysis. Many information goods and services require time to consume and, as a result, require that the opportunity cost to patrons or users be considered in calculating demand for them. Faster service in delivering information goods may not always result in additional revenue for the library, government agency, or organization, however, it does provide a measurable benefit to patrons, users, and consumers.

Future costs and benefits must be discounted to determine their present value. Benefits that consumers must wait for are not worth as much today and therefore must be discounted. The present value of any purchase of a durable good is the discounted value of the stream of future benefits and costs to the consumer.

Discussion Questions

1. Consider the following goods and services: photocopying, requesting an article from interlibrary loan, going to a movie, and buying a magazine. Discuss how the opportunity cost of time is important in each case.

2. Consider the difference between seeing a movie in a theater, renting the movie on videotape, and seeing it on television. How does the opportunity cost of time make a difference between how you choose to consume the movie? How does its present value influence this? How can movie distributors use this information to maximize profits?

3. Describe the methodology of a study to investigate the value of charging user fees for the Internet. How do transaction costs of user fees fit into your study?

4. Consider the differences between sending a letter by first class mail, overnight delivery, fax, and electronic mail. How would you measure the opportunity cost of each alternative method of sending information.

Notes

1. Jeff E. Biddle and Daniel S. Hamermesh, "Sleep and the Allocation of Time," *Journal of Political Economy* (1990): 922-43.

2. Malcolm Getz, "Some Benefits of the Online Catalog," *College & Research Libraries* 48, no. 3 (1987): 224-40; Malcolm Getz, "More Benefits of Automation," *College & Research Libraries* 49, no. 6 (1988): 534-44.

3. Hal R. Varian and Jeffrey K. Mackie-Mason, "Some Economics of the Internet" working paper, University of Michigan Center for Research on Economic and Social Theory, 1993: 93-116.

Resource Sharing

Books, journals, newspapers, CD-ROMs, videotapes, and movies are information resources that can be shared. In each case, when buyers share their purchases with others or agree to jointly purchase a good, they are resource sharing. When an academic library participates in interlibrary loan, it is resource sharing. In fact, any library, whether public or private, academic or corporate, is sharing information resources, and is an organization whose cooperative agreements can produce more efficient purchase and consumption policies. In each case, these information resources can be modeled as public goods.

Unfortunately, not all organizations or consumers who engage in resource sharing do so efficiently. Libraries in consortia do not always use cooperative collection development strategies. They see resource sharing as a way to increase access to materials the library does not own, rather than a way to cooperatively lower costs by decreasing duplicate materials. Whether the materials shared are journal subscriptions, compact discs, or personal computers, understanding the economic benefits and costs of sharing information resources is important for managers and policymakers.

Multiple Users of Information Resources

Resource sharing is defined as using information goods or services as public goods, meaning they are shared among users. Each consumer or user receives a benefit from the collectively shared individual good. The collective benefit to all users is the public good benefit or demand for that good. Efficient resource sharing implies using the collective benefit as a measure of social benefit and comparing this to the marginal cost of production and delivery.

153

Journal subscriptions and books and the interlibrary loan of these resources at academic libraries are excellent examples of resource sharing. Each library purchases journal subscriptions and books to satisfy the collective needs of their patrons. Use studies, citation analysis, and faculty and student requests are all used to determine the potential value of different journals and books so the library can make efficient decisions about purchasing them.

If patrons ask for books or journals their library does not own, the library will request to borrow it from a library that owns this journal or book. In this way the purchases of one library are shared with other libraries. However, when one library purchases a book or journal title, it only considers the benefits to its own patrons and not the possible benefits to patrons of other libraries. A broader definition of economic efficiency would require that the benefit to all patrons be considered. An economic analysis of consortia considers the benefits provided to all library patrons within the consortium, not only the benefit to patrons of any individual library. In other words, economic efficiency for the consortium, which considers the needs of all patrons, may differ from efficient acquisitions and interlibrary loan policy for an individual library within the consortium.

To show this, figure 12.1 illustrates the economics of a library's decision to subscribe to a journal. The demand for use or marginal social benefit of a particular year's subscription for this particular journal is curve MSB. The marginal cost of access to this journal through document delivery is shown in curve MC_{DD}. While use, represented on the horizontal axis, should be the present value of use, for simplicity the assumption will be made that future uses and present uses are of equal value. Assume that patrons are equally satisfied with articles that they acquire directly through the library and articles received from interlibrary loan through document delivery. The initial assumption will also be that there is no difference in the opportunity cost of patron access using a library subscription or using document delivery.

If the library subscribes to this journal, the benefit of a subscription is the consumer surplus (area ABC) that patrons receive from the subscription. Because patrons have a price of zero to access the journal when the library owns the subscription, their level of use is Q. Let S equal the cost of the subscription, which is the fixed costs of subscribing to the journal and the marginal costs of individual use. Then the net economic benefit equals (ABC - S).

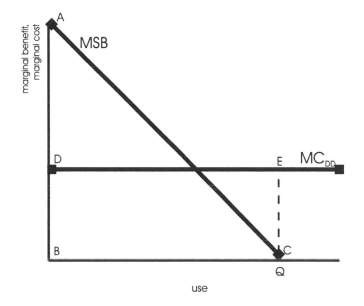

Figure 12.1. Value of a Journal Subscription to an Individual Library.

Most academic libraries provide free interlibrary loan services to patrons. Patrons can receive a copy of most articles from academic journals without charge. However, while patrons are not charged for these services, there are real costs to the library of delivering articles. If figure 12.1 represents the use or demand for articles from this journal—assuming there is no change in use whether access is provided by interlibrary loan or a journal subscription—then the benefit from "free" interlibrary loan is the consumer surplus ABC. Given the cost of interlibrary loan to the library of $Q(MC_{DD})$, the net benefit of access through interlibrary loan is: $[ABC - Q(MC_{DD})]$. Then the difference between the net benefit of a journal subscription and access through interlibrary loan is

$$(ABC - S) - [ABC - Q(MC_{DD})] = [Q(MC) - S] \qquad (12.1)$$

Equation 12.1 shows that the difference between the net benefit of a journal subscription and interlibrary loan is simply the difference in their costs. This assumes that there is no difference in the level of use between interlibrary loan and a journal subscription. This is an assumption used by Palmour, et al. (1977), Getz (1991), and Kingma (1994).[1] In this case, it is not necessary to measure the benefits to patrons of access to determine which method is more economically efficient; only the measurement of costs of delivery is needed. Let

C = Q (MC) - S. Then if C is positive, a journal subscription costs less than interlibrary loan access, and it is economically efficient for the library to subscribe to the journal. If C is negative, a journal subscription costs more than interlibrary loan access and it is economically efficient for the library to provide access to the journal through interlibrary loan.

In this example, economic efficiency results from the method of access that is more cost-efficient. The cost-efficiency of a journal subscription relative to document delivery of journal articles depends on the costs of each method of access and the expected level of use of the particular journal title. If there is sufficient use for a journal, it will be more cost efficient to provide access by purchasing a subscription. The importance of use in this equation is illustrated in figure 12.2.

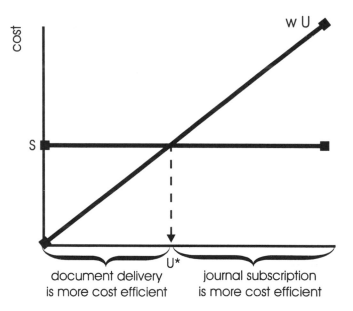

Figure 12.2. Cost-Efficiency of Access Versus Ownership.

Figure 12.2 shows the total cost of both methods of access. In figure 12.2, the cost of a journal subscription (S) is the subscription price plus any other costs associated with the subscription. The total cost of document delivery (wU), equals the marginal cost (w) per document or article delivered times the number of requests (U). U* is the break-even level of requests. If use is below U*, access is more efficiently provided through interlibrary loan. If use is greater than U*, access is more efficiently provided through a journal subscription.

While libraries do not always consider the economic efficiency of interlibrary loan and journal subscription policy, economics certainly influences their use of interlibrary loan. As journal prices increase or the cost of interlibrary loan decreases, interlibrary loan offers greater financial savings to the library. The influence of an increase in journal subscription prices is illustrated in figure 12.3. In figure 12.3, the price of a journal subscription increases from S to S'. As a result, the break-even level of use increases from U to U'. As journal subscription prices increase, there is a larger range of use in which it is more cost efficient to offer access through interlibrary loan.

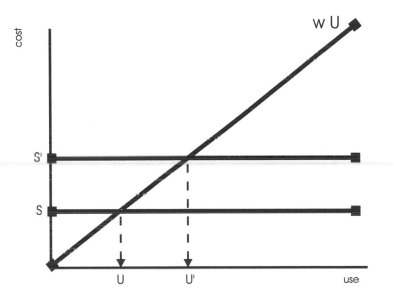

Figure 12.3. A Change in Journal Subscription Price.

Interlibrary loan is, by definition, a consortium arrangement among participating libraries. Library networks and commercial document delivery services provide low-cost access to journals for patrons who otherwise would be denied access to them.

Many libraries also form smaller consortia of local libraries or libraries with complementary journal collections. These consortia are economically efficient only if they deliver lower cost or higher quality access to journal articles than that available through existing interlibrary loan networks. If this occurs, then cooperative collection development among partners in the consortium can result in an increase in economic efficiency. If joint collection development is used, individual libraries in the consortium that might not currently subscribe to a particular journal may subscribe once the benefits to the consortium are recognized. Joint collection development essentially treats the collection of the consortium as a single large collection. The decision for the consortium to subscribe to a particular journal is illustrated in figure 12.4.

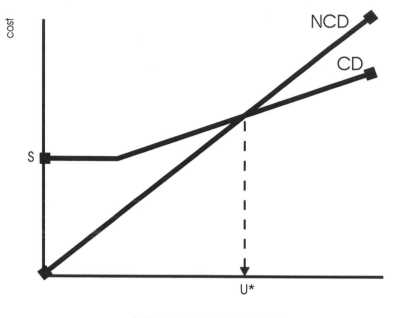

Figure 12.4. Consortium Ownership.

Figure 12.4 represents the costs of access to a particular journal title through consortium and non-consortium document delivery. The horizontal axis in figure 12.4 is the total use of this journal by all member libraries. The total cost of access through non-consortium document delivery (NCD) is the marginal cost of delivery times the total number of requests by all member libraries. The total cost of access through the consortium (CD) is the cost of the journal subscription (S) to the consortium plus the cost of article delivery to other members of the consortium. The cost of article delivery to the other members of the consortium is the marginal cost of delivery within the consortium times the level of use by all members who do not own the journal subscription.

Figure 12.4 assumes that no library within the consortium is already subscribing to this particular journal. What is illustrated in figure 12.4 is the financial advantage to the consortium of subscribing to a particular journal that no individual library would subscribe to otherwise. In this case, the break-even point is U*. If the sum of use by all member libraries exceeds U*, it is economically efficient for the consortium to subscribe to this journal. If total use is less than U*, it is more efficient to use higher cost non-consortium delivery.

While it is easy to illustrate the financial savings to a library consortium, it is more difficult to operate a consortium efficiently and provide appropriate incentives for efficient collective decisions. For example, the one library that will subscribe to the journal in figure 12.4 has no financial incentive to do so even though total consortium use exceeds U*. This is because the single library would not subscribe to the journal if it were not part of the consortium. As a result, individual libraries must make decisions that serve the consortium's best interests but not their own best interests. While it is more cost-efficient for the consortium to behave as a single large library, unless library budgets are controlled by a single consortium manager, individual library managers will be concerned with their own library's budget and not with the resource needs of other members of the consortium.

The Research Libraries Network (RLN) has attempted to answer the consortium financing problem by compensating libraries that are excessive lenders of materials over RLN. If a library lends more than it borrows, it receives a refund based on net lending. This rewards individual libraries that may have collections valued by the rest of the members of RLN, and provides an incentive for them to consider the resource needs of other libraries when making their collections decisions.

The Opportunity Cost of Patron Time

When resources are shared among libraries, agencies, or individuals, there is usually a waiting period for the borrower. For example, when a library uses interlibrary loan to provide patrons with access to journal articles, the patron must wait a few days or weeks to get the requested article. The cost of the time spent waiting must be included when determining the economic cost of interlibrary loan.

Figure 12.5 shows the full economic costs and benefits of providing journal access to patrons through interlibrary loan versus a journal subscription. In figure 12.5, t_{DD} is the opportunity cost of time spent by the patron waiting for an article to be delivered by interlibrary loan; t_{own} is the opportunity cost of time spent by the patron retrieving an article from a journal in the library; and MC_{DD} is the marginal cost of document delivery, including staff time, supplies, and document delivery charges. Figure 12.5 assumes that the opportunity cost of time for a patron waiting for an article to be delivered through interlibrary loan is greater than the value of the time spent retrieving a journal article if the library owned the subscription.

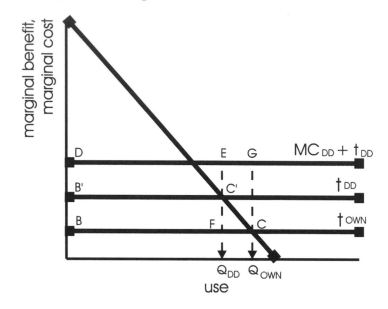

Figure 12.5. Opportunity Cost of Access Through Subscription Versus Interlibrary Loan.

If the library owns the subscription, the level of use is Q_{own} and the consumer surplus from this use is equal to area ABC. The net benefit is (ABC-S) where S is the fixed cost of the subscription. If the library does not own the subscription and patrons are not charged for interlibrary loan, the level of requests for articles is Q_{DD} where the marginal value of a patron's time, t_{DD}, just equals the marginal benefit to the patron of receiving the article. In this case, the consumer surplus is AB'C'. The net benefit from using interlibrary loan is the consumer surplus minus the costs of inter-library loan, [AB'C' - (MC_{DD}) Q_{DD}]. The difference in net benefit between providing access through a journal subscription and interlibrary loan is

$$ABC - S - [AB'C' - (MC_{DD})Q_{DD}] = BCC'B' + (MC_{DD})Q_{DD} - S \quad (12.2)$$

The right-hand side of equation 12.2 is the value of the consumer surplus gained from purchasing the subscription (BCC'B') plus the cost of interlibrary loan [$(MC_{DD})Q_{DD}$] that will be saved if the library purchases a subscription, minus the cost of the subscription (S). The difference between equation 12.2 and equation 12.1 (page 155) is that the value of the opportunity cost of time for the patron is included in equation 12.2. If a library subscribes to a journal, the patron gains area BCC'B' in consumer surplus from more immediate access to journal articles.

While it is possible to illustrate the net benefit of access versus ownership of journal articles, it is more difficult to actually estimate this difference. A library may know the number of articles requested through interlibrary loan from a particular journal, but this does not necessarily indicate the level of use the journal would receive if the library subscribed to it. Similarly, a library may have statistics on the number of patrons who benefit from a journal subscription, but this does not indicate the number of articles that would be requested using interlibrary loan if the library did not subscribe to the journal. As a result, it is difficult to estimate the difference between Q_{DD} and Q_{own} and the area of BCC'B'.

The value of the area BCC'B' can be approximated if information on the value of a patron's time spent waiting for an article to be delivered (t_{DD}) and time spent when the library subscribes to the journal (t_{own}) can be determined. Using figure 12.5, if the library only has statistics on the number of requests for a particular journal through interlibrary loan, then the value of area BCC'B' can be estimated using Q_{DD} (t_{DD} - t_{own}), the number of requests using interlibrary loan multiplied by the difference in the opportunity cost of time. In this case, the error between the estimate and the actual net benefit of a journal subscription is area FCC' in figure 12.5. Using the number of articles requested from a journal through interlibrary loan underestimates the net benefit of the library owning a subscription; the size of the error depends on the difference in patron use of interlibrary loan and a journal subscription. If, using this approximation, equation 12.2 is positive, then the library definitely should subscribe to this journal.

Alternatively, the level of use of a journal on the shelf can be used to estimate the value of area BCC'B'. In this case, BCC'B' can be approximated as Q_{own} (t_{DD} - t_{own}). From figure 12.5, this overestimates the value of a journal subscription by area EGCC'. This approximation underestimates the value of using interlibrary loan for this particular journal subscription, where the size of the error depends on the difference in patron use of interlibrary loan and a journal subscription. If, using this approximation, equation 12.2 is negative, then the library definitely should use interlibrary loan to provide access to this journal.

Summary

The economic efficiency of resource sharing depends on the level of use of shared resources, their cost, and the opportunity cost of patrons waiting for delivery. Resource sharing can provide economically efficient access for library consortia; however, the difficulties of providing incentives to share and purchase shared resources must be overcome. In addition, while resource sharing can be cost-efficient for libraries, the opportunity cost to patrons of waiting for shared resources must be considered to determine if it is economically efficient for patrons.

Resource sharing for academic libraries has increased as a result of the increases in journal prices. While the potential savings for library consortia that share journal subscriptions have been described, there may also be an effect on the market for journal subscriptions and prices, which has not been explored. As libraries continue to share their resources, the result may be that journal prices rise further to offset the decline in subscriptions or that publishers simply stop publishing some journal titles. However, the aggregate effect of journal cancellations is less important to individual libraries than the potential savings from sharing individual journals.

Discussion Questions

1. If there were no external benefits from use, how would imposing user fees for interlibrary loan increase economic efficiency? If the university felt there was an external benefit for the patron in receiving an article through interlibrary loan, what user fees should be imposed? Explain.

2. Some libraries feel that while the consortium may not deliver articles at a lower cost, the "spirit of cooperation" produced by the consortium makes it worthwhile. Comment.

3. How does the opportunity cost of time influence the efficiency of consortium delivery?

4. Draw the demand and cost curves for subscriptions to an individual journal title. (To simplify this, assume that publishers charge the same price to every subscriber.) As libraries increase resource sharing, what effect does this have on this diagram? Draw the demand and supply for subscriptions to all academic journals. What happens in this market as libraries increase their resource sharing? How can you explain the differences between these two diagrams?

Note

1. Vernon E. Palmour, Marcia C. Bellassai, and Robert R. V. Wiederkehr, *Costs of Owning, Borrowing, and Disposing of Periodical Publications* (Arlington, VA: Center for Naval Analysis, 1977): Malcolm Getz, "Economics: Document Delivery," *The Bottom Line* 5 (Winter 1991-1992): 40-44; and Bruce R. Kingma, "Access to Journal Articles: An Economic Model of Document Delivery and Library Resource Sharing," *American Society for Information Science Conference Proceedings* 30 (1994): 8-16.

Cost-Benefit Analysis

Whether purchasing a new photocopy machine or computer, hiring an additional employee, or determining the most efficient method of document delivery, cost-benefit analysis enables managers and policymakers to quantify the costs and benefits of their alternatives. Therefore it provides the tools to make better management decisions.

Calculating costs requires data on prices, wages, and other financial costs and opportunity costs. Data on prices, wages, and other financial costs are usually readily available; however, calculating the opportunity costs and the present value of future costs can be more difficult to measure. A photocopier costs more than the purchase price. Future maintenance costs must be paid for, as well as opportunity costs incurred by patrons. An employee costs more than the sum of the wages and benefits. The opportunity cost of an employee includes the time spent training and managing the employee. Even volunteer labor has an opportunity cost, including the cost of managing, supervising, and training.

Calculating consumer benefits requires data on the level of use, the price paid, and the opportunity cost spent acquiring a good or service. Benefits include consumer surplus, added revenues or profit, increased employee productivity, and can even include the "warm-glow" benefit that volunteers receive from helping a worthy cause. Measuring consumer surplus requires estimating the demand or willingness-to-pay of consumers or patrons.

The first step in cost-benefit analysis is determining who are the stakeholders that benefit and pay for a project. The second step is to identify the costs and benefits for each stakeholder group. Finally, costs and benefits for each stakeholder group must be measured to show which groups have a net benefit or net cost and whether the total benefits for the project exceed the total costs.

The Matrix of Benefits and Costs

The stakeholders in a cost-benefit analysis are the individuals or groups who incur costs or receive benefits from the project. Stakeholders can be taxpayers, clients, patrons, employees, volunteers, or government agencies. Identifying the stakeholder groups, and the costs and benefits for each group, enables a decision maker to build a matrix of stakeholders and their costs and benefits.

Consider the costs and benefits of a children's reading program at a local public library. The stakeholders are the children, their parents, the program volunteers, the library, and the other members of the community. The children who participate in this program will benefit by gaining better reading skills, entertainment, and better education. The children's cost is the opportunity cost of the time they spend in the program. The parents benefit from the value of the service provided to their children and from having their children looked after for a period of time. The parents' costs are the opportunity cost of the time spent driving the children to and from the public library and the time spent waiting for the children while they are participating in the program. Given that the program is staffed by volunteers, the cost to the volunteer is the opportunity cost of the volunteer's time. Because volunteers participate in this program without financial compensation, they must receive some benefit to compensate them for the opportunity cost of their time. Volunteers receive "warm-glow" or psychic value from volunteering. In addition, they gain experience working in a library that may lead to a paid job. Other costs and benefits include the library's costs of supplies or space to run the program and the community's benefit of better educated children.

The community may also have to pay for this program with tax revenues; however, these tax revenues are transfer payments. *Transfer payments* are an exchange of revenue from one group in society to another that does not result in a net increase or decrease in societal benefits. In this case, the tax revenues that appear as a cost to the community result in a benefit of an equal amount to the library. Table 13.1 shows the complete matrix of costs and benefit from the library reading program.

Estimating Costs and Benefits

While the costs and benefits to individual stakeholders can be described, it is more difficult to quantify these costs and benefits. First, it is important to understand that some of the costs in table 13.1 are financial costs, while others are opportunity costs of an individual's time. The opportunity costs of a volunteer's time is a real cost to the volunteer and important in the economic analysis; however, it does not represent a financial cost to the library.

Table 13.1.
Sample Matrix of Benefits and Costs for Children's Reading Program

	Stakeholders			
	Community	Volunteers	Children & Parents	Library
Costs				
Wages				X
Space				X
Opportunity cost of time		X	X	
Supplies				X
Benefits				
Educated children	X		X	
Future library users			X	X
Child care			X	
"Warm-glow"	X	X		X
Transfer Payments				
Taxes	X			X
Charges			X	X
Total				

Calculation of the opportunity cost of volunteers' time can be arrived at by using the after-tax market wage rate as an approximation of what an hour of time is worth to volunteers. Volunteers forgo the amount they could have earned as paid laborers, for which they would have received their wage minus income and payroll taxes. While this may not be precisely how volunteers value their time, it is a reasonable approximation. If it takes two hours of preparation, driving, and reading for each story hour, and volunteers would earn $10 per hour at an equivalent paid job, then the opportunity cost of their time is $20 for each story hour. A series of 10 story hours would cost volunteers $200 in time. Given that the benefit of volunteering must be worth at least as much as the opportunity cost of time spent volunteering it can be said that the benefit volunteers receive is $200+ for the series of 10 story hours.

Parents and children incur opportunity costs from driving to and from story hour. Assume that there are 10 children who come to each of 10 story hours. If parents have an average opportunity cost of time of $10 and it takes an average of 1.5 hours to drive to and attend each story hour, then the opportunity cost to parents is $1,500. Because parents are willing to bring their children only if the value of their participation is greater than the cost, the benefit to the parents must be $1,500+. Therefore, parents, on average, are willing to pay $10 per child per story hour of opportunity costs for educational programs such as story hours. In addition, there is the value of one hour of child care for each of 10 children. If the standard payment for baby-sitters is $5 per hour, the value of this care can be approximated at $500 for the 10 children for 10 story hours. Finally, there is the benefit parents receive from providing their children and themselves with exposure to and familiarity with the local public library. In table 13.2 this is approximated as $500.

Parents may also have to incur a user fee to participate in the program. According to table 13.2, if parents were charged a user fee they would be willing to pay a total of $500 or $5 per story hour per child. This $500 is the parents' benefit of $2,000 minus their opportunity cost of $1,500 for the story hours. If the library charges a user fee for the story hour it would be a transfer payment from the parents to the library, representing no net gain or loss in the cost-benefit table. However, implementing a user fee would enable the community to use these tax revenues to pay for other community services.

Table 13.2.
Actual Matrix of Benefits and Costs for Children's Reading Program

	Stakeholders			
	Community	Volunteers	Children & Parents	Library
Costs				
Wages				($100)
Space				($100)
Opportunity cost of time		($200)	($1,500)	
Supplies				($100)
Benefits				
Educated children	+		$1,000	
Future library users			$500	+
Child care			$500	
"Warm-glow"	+	$200+		+
Transfer payments				
Taxes	($300)			$300
Charges			+	+
Total	($300)	+	$500	+

The library and community also incur benefits and costs. According to table 13.2, the story hours may have a financial cost of $300 to the library, the sum of $100 for library staff wages to administer the program, $100 for the cost of the library space, and $100 for supplies such as brochures and handouts. The library receives $300 in taxes from the community to pay for this. This $300 is a benefit to the library but a cost to the community. However, the community receives the "warm-glow" benefit of assisting the program and the benefit of more educated children in the community, although both types of benefits are difficult to quantify. Parents, children, and volunteers are also part of the community, and they receive additional benefits, although their costs and benefits are listed separately in table 13.2. The library also receives the "warm-glow" benefits and the benefit of future library users who are more likely to support the library and bring their own children to the library when they get older.

In total, table 13.2 shows that the $500 in benefits to children and parents plus other benefits that are more difficult to measure, outweigh the $300 in taxes to the community.

Present Value

Frequently, the costs and benefits of a program occur over several years. Examples of this include purchasing books and journals that are expect to last several years, purchasing durable equipment such as new computers, photocopy machines, desks, or shelving, and building new buildings. In each case there is a different anticipated life span of the durable purchase. Personal computers may have a relatively short life span of two or three years before they become obsolete, while new shelving may be used for 10 years or more.

Table 13.3 shows the cost-benefit matrix for building a new library. The stakeholders for a new library include the community, the library users, and the library staff and administration including the library director, board, and employees. The taxes paid by the community are a transfer from the community to the library. A more detailed cost-benefit analysis would include the deadweight loss from these taxes as an additional cost; however, this deadweight loss would depend on the type of taxes used—sales, property, income, or other. The community benefits from the library because the general population is better educated and therefore its citizens are able to make better decisions within the community. In addition, children spending time at the library become more productive, responsible adults.

Library users incur opportunity costs from travel to and use of the library, and receive benefits from books, journals, and other information sources. The library has costs of maintenance, building, materials, and salaries. Without significant user fees, these costs are paid for with local tax revenue.

Table 13.3.
Cost-Benefit Matrix for Building a New Library

	Stakeholders		
	Community	Library Users	Library
Present Value of Costs			
Materials & construction			X
Annual salaries & maintenance			X
Opportunity cost of use & travel to the library		X	
Present Value of Benefits			
Better educated population	X		
Value of information		X	
Transfers			
Taxes	X		X
Total			

While each of the costs and benefits in table 13.3 are important, the most significant pieces of this matrix are the financial costs of the building, salaries, and materials and the benefits library patrons receive from using it. The costs of building a library are incurred within the initial year of construction, while salaries, maintenance, and the costs of materials are incurred over the lifetime of the library. To estimate these costs, data on the actual costs for similar-sized libraries can be collected.

The benefits that library patrons receive are more difficult to quantify. Data on the population of the user community, the use of other local libraries, and the use of libraries by communities of similar size and socioeconomic status can be used to estimate patron use for the library. However, library use does not perfectly translate into the benefit patrons receive from the library. Surveys of library patrons' willingness-to-pay for library services and demand analysis of library use in similar communities can be used to predict the value of library services. As this calculation predicts the annual benefit of the library, the present value of the benefit must be calculated based on the expected life span of the library.

An alternative way to determine if the benefits of a new library are worth the costs is to divide the present value of costs by the anticipated number of users to determine the minimum benefit necessary per patron to make the library economically viable. Of course, local voters are usually the ultimate judges about whether the benefits a community receives from a library are greater than the costs.

Common Mistakes in Cost-Benefit Analysis

There are several potential pitfalls in using cost-benefit analysis to determine the worth of a project. These result from the inability of the analyst to clearly determine and quantify the costs and benefits of a project. As a result, benefits or costs may be counted more than once, or items that seem to be a benefit to one group are not seen as such to another group.

The Double Counting Game

One of the most common mistakes in cost-benefit analysis is double counting. This happens when benefits are counted more than once. The example used in table 13.2 can be used to illustrate this. The benefits of child care and the benefits of the education that the children received were both included as overall benefits of the library story hour program. If one were to estimate the benefit that the children received as equivalent to the cost parents would be willing to pay comparable commercially run programs, then these benefits would also include the value of child care. Therefore, adding child care as a separate benefit of the library reading program would "double count" the benefit of child care.

Frequently the double counting game occurs when an analyst counts the value to a community of a project plus the increase in property values. This might occur if the analyst were to count both the value to the community of a new library and the higher property values in communities with high-quality public libraries. The increase in property value would measure the value of a high-quality public library to individuals, considering a move to that community. Therefore, the value should not be added to the value that current citizens might be willing to pay for a new library.

The Labor Game

A second common error in cost-benefit analysis is counting the wages and salaries of employees as benefits rather than costs. Salaries and wages are expenditures resulting from a project. The salaries and wages that an individual receives may seem like a benefit to that person, but employees are providing their services in exchange for payment. Hiring one more person to work at a new library or new government information service means that the individual is not working at another job in another sector of the economy. This is a common mistake made by government analysts when advertising the benefits of a government project.

Summary

Cost-benefit analysis can be effectively used to determine whether projects and policies are economically worthwhile. The matrix of costs and benefits helps the analyst determine the groups that receive benefits and incur costs from a project. Data on costs, use, and value can be used to quantify the costs and benefits. This and preceding chapters have provided an introduction to cost-benefit analysis, showing the important economic concepts and components, illustrating how to begin such an analysis, and identifying the common problems that occur.

Discussion Questions

1. Consider a project at your organization. Create a cost-benefit matrix for this project. Can you estimate the value of the costs and benefits in this matrix? What additional data would you need to do so?

2. Because patrons do not usually pay to use the library, it is difficult to measure their consumer surplus from it. Describe a project that might help you estimate the consumer surplus of library use. If you had data on patron wages, the number of times they used the library, and how much time they spend in the library, how could you use this to estimate their consumer surplus from library use?

3. A corporation is considering building a technical library to support its researchers. Create a cost-benefit matrix for this special library. How might you estimate the value of this library?

Appendix A:
Marginal, Average, and Total Costs: More Practice

The mathematical concepts of marginal, average, and total values (benefits or costs) are critical to understanding economic analysis. To help provide a clearer understanding of these concepts, table A.1 and figure A.1 illustrate the marginal, total, and average costs of a child's birthday party.

Table A.1.
The Costs of a Birthday Party

Number of Children Attending	Marginal Cost per Child	Total Cost	Average Cost per Child
1	$99	$99	$99.00
2	$0	$99	$49.50
3	$0	$99	$33.00
4	$0	$99	$24.75
5	$0	$99	$19.80
6	$0	$99	$16.50
7	$0	$99	$14.14
8	$0	$99	$12.38
9	$0	$99	$11.00
10	$0	$99	$9.90
11	$0	$99	$9.00
12	$0	$99	$8.25
13	$10	$109	$8.38
14	$10	$119	$8.50
15	$10	$129	$8.60
16	$10	$139	$8.69
17	$10	$149	$8.76
18	$10	$159	$8.83
19	$30	$189	$9.95

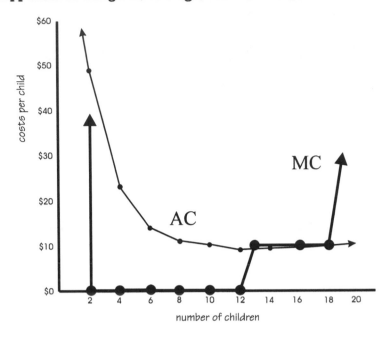

Figure A.1. Marginal and Average Costs of a Birthday Party.

Children's playlands that provide, for a fee, children's birthday parties are becoming more and more popular. Birthday parties at children's playlands usually have a fixed cost for a maximum number of children. After that maximum is reached, there is an additional charge per additional child. Table A.1 represents the costs for a fictitious child's birthday party. Assume that the cost of the party is $99 for up to 12 children. There is an additional charge of $10 per child beyond the first 12 for the extra pizza, cake, and party goodies. In addition, if 19 or more children attend the party, there is an additional charge of $20 for the additional playland staff member to supervise the party. Assume that there are 19 children that could be invited to the party.

The marginal cost of each additional child is shown in the second column of table A.1. Remember, the *marginal value* of something is the additional value of the next unit. Therefore, the marginal cost of the first child is $99, which must be paid regardless of how many children attend the party. Because there is no additional charge for the second through 12th child, their marginal cost is zero. The marginal cost of the 13th through 18th children is $10 per child. The 19th child has a marginal cost of $30, the $10 for the additional cake, pizza, and party goodies plus the $20 for the additional playland staff supervisor.

Total cost is the sum of the marginal costs. The total cost for a party of 12 or less is $99. Adding a ninth child to the party of eight adds a marginal cost of zero, so the total cost remains the same. When the party grows beyond 12 children, total cost increases by the marginal cost of each additional child.

The *average cost* is the total cost divided by the number of children. As the number of children increases up to 12 children, the average cost per child decreases. As the 13th child is added, the additional cost of $10 per child increases the average cost per child.

How can this cost information be used to determine the optimal size of a party? The marginal cost gives the additional cost per child. In determining whether or not to invite an additional child to the party, the marginal cost indicates how much that child will cost. Assume each child brings a present worth $9.50 to the party. In this case, the marginal cost of the 13th child exceeds the marginal benefit (the value of the present they are bringing) and only 12 children will be invited to the party. If the expected value of a present is $20, then the first 18 children will be invited to the party but the 19th will not.

The average cost per child is not used to decide how many children to invite to the party. It is only used to determine the "cost per child," or the average net benefit per child, and to calculate the net "profit" from the party. For example, if the expected value of a present is $9.50 per child, at least 11 children must be invited for the average benefit to exceed the average cost. At 11 children invited, the birthday child will receive more in total gifts—($9.50 per gift) x (11 gifts) = $104.50— than the total cost of the party ($99). The net "profit" from a party of 11 children equals the number of children times the difference between the marginal benefit, or the average expected value of a gift ($9.50), and the average cost per child ($9), 11 x $0.50 = $5.50.

Discussion Questions

1. Assume that more than 19 children can be invited to the party. Calculate the total, marginal, and average cost per child for a party of up to 30 children. Assume that the expected value of a gift is $20 per child. How many children will be invited to the party?

Appendix B: Measuring the Value of Sex Education

To formally model the value of sex education, the costs of unsafe behavior and the impact of sex education on those who receive it must be measured and evaluated. For the purposes of this example, several assumptions about the effects of unsafe behavior and education will be made. First, assume that everyone who receives sex education practices safe sex and has a 0 percent chance of contracting a sexually transmitted disease (STD). Assume that everyone who does not practice safe sex has a 0.01 percent chance of getting an STD. If, on average, the value of the lost productivity, wages, and loss of life resulting from someone getting an STD is $1,000,000, then the average expected benefit from practicing safe sex is the probability of getting an STD times the loss if contracted, or 0.0001 x $1,000,000 = $100.

As the number of people getting the necessary education increases, there are fewer people without the education and fewer cases of STDs being contracted. This means that the probability of an uneducated person contracting an STD decreases and the expected marginal benefit of the education decreases. This is shown in the decreasing marginal benefit curve (MB), or demand curve, in figure 5.4, on page 66. The more others are educated the less likely the uneducated are to contract a disease, thus lowering the value of the education to them.

What is the cost of an education? First, assume that the financial cost of printing and mailing brochures is trivial. In this case, the opportunity cost or willingness of individuals to spend the time and effort to be educated on such matters is the major impediment to this type of information. If one assumes that the average individual gets paid $15 per hour and it takes two hours to find, read, and comprehend the information on safe sex, then the opportunity cost of this education is $30 (calculating the value of time is described in more detail in chapter 11). Individuals will become educated as long as the expected marginal benefit of the education exceeds their marginal cost. This establishes the equilibrium level of education at Q* in figure 5.4.

While it is difficult to believe that individuals actually calculate the value of their time and the benefit of the education, the equilibrium level of education exists. There are those who place a value on this type of education that exceeds the value of the time they must spend to receive it. Similarly, there are those who do not receive this type of education because their perceived value of it is less than the time and effort it would take for them to receive and understand it. As a result, people become educated or remain uneducated based on their perceived value (marginal benefit) and their perceived cost (marginal cost) of the education.

Finally, assume that once someone contracts an STD, they have a 0.001 percent chance of infecting someone else. Then the value of the positive externality from someone practicing safe sex is the value of preventing others from becoming infected. This equals the probability of infecting someone else times the value of the lost productivity, wages, or loss of life 0.00001 x $1,000,000 = $10, which is now prevented with an education. This is the marginal external benefit (MEB) curve in figure 5.3. The sum of the marginal benefit curve and the marginal external benefit curve is the marginal social benefit (MSB) curve in figure 5.4. The intersection of the marginal social benefit curve and the marginal cost curve establishes the socially efficient level of education at Q. Q is located to the right of Q*, the market equilibrium, which is the intersection of MB and MC. Therefore, too few people are receiving the education to meet the socially efficient level of sex education.

A subsidy equal to the marginal external benefit of $10 will "internalize" the externality by encouraging people to get the education and will produce the socially optimal level of education of Q. The subsidy can take the form of paying people $10 to read the sex education literature, or making it more convenient to get information through public service announcements on television or radio, or making sex education mandatory in schools or the workplace. However, as noted in chapter 5, the positive externality of this type of education for some may be a negative externality for others. Therefore, policy used to correct the effects of a positive externality must be carefully crafted to avoid increasing a negative externality for others.

Appendix C:
Ramsey Prices and Economic Efficiency

In the example presented in chapter 10, figures 10.7 and 10.8, increasing the cost of library photocopies by $0.01 resulted in $1,000 of deadweight loss and $10,000 in additional benefit gained by library patrons. If the price of photocopies in the library were to continue to increase, additional deadweight loss would be incurred while additional reference librarians could be hired. How much should the price of a photocopy be increased?

Any increase in the price above marginal cost will result in deadweight loss, and the purchase of any good with a marginal benefit above marginal cost will result in a net benefit gain. In setting prices above marginal cost, it is important to ensure that the deadweight loss caused from raising surplus revenue is always less than the marginal benefit gained spending that revenue on other goods and services.

The *efficiency-loss ratio* is defined as the ratio of deadweight loss to net revenue gained. In the example shown in figure 10.7, the efficiency-loss ratio is ABC/BCDE or $1,000/$20,000, or $0.05. This means that there is $0.05 of deadweight loss for every $1 of revenue gained from increasing the price of a photocopy. The *benefit-cost ratio* is defined as the ratio of marginal benefit to marginal cost. In the example shown in figure 10.8, the benefit-cost ratio is $30,000/$20,000, or 1.5. This means that there is $1.50 of benefit for every $1 spent on hiring reference librarians. In this example, library patrons were made better off by increasing photocopy prices and using the surplus revenue to hire an additional reference librarian. In other words, for every dollar raised to purchase reference librarian services, there was a consumer surplus loss to patrons of $1.05 ($1 in revenue plus $0.05 in deadweight loss). That $1.05 surplus purchased $1.50 in new benefit.

As long as the benefit patrons receive is greater than the loss, the price of photocopying should be increased and additional revenues should be used to purchase reference librarian services. In other words, the price of a photocopy should be increased as long as the efficiency-loss ratio plus 1 is less than the benefit-cost ratio.

As the price of a photocopy increases, the deadweight loss increases while the gain in net revenues decreases, thereby increasing the efficiency-loss ratio. Similarly, as the number of reference librarians employed increases, the marginal benefit of an additional reference librarian will decrease, reducing the benefit-cost ratio. This is demonstrated in figure C.1.

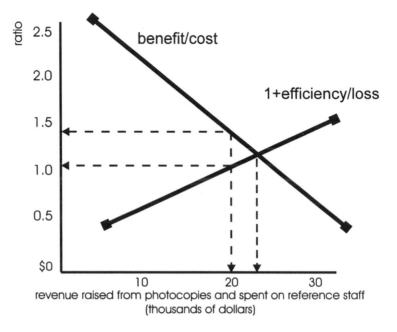

Figure C.1. Optimal Photocopy Price.

Ultimately, the efficiency-loss ratio plus 1 will equal the benefit-cost ratio at point A in figure C.1. At this point, any further increase in the price of a photocopy will result in more consumer surplus lost from photocopying than the increase in net benefit from hiring an additional reference librarian.

Bibliography

Akerlof, George A. "The Market for 'Lemons': Quality Uncertainty and the Market Mechanism." *Quarterly Journal of Economics* 84, no. 3 (August 1970): 488-500.

Alchian, A., and Harold Demsetz. "Production, Information Costs, and Economic Organization." *American Economic Review* 65, no. 5 (December 1972): 777-95.

Alexander, Peter J. "Entry Barriers, Release Behavior, and Multi-Product Firms in the Music Recording Industry." *Review of Industrial Organization* 9, no. 1 (1994): 85-98.

Allen, Beth. "Information as an Economic Commodity." *American Economic Review* 80, no. 2 (May 1990): 268-73.

Antonelli, Cristiano. "Information Technology and the Derived Demand for Telecommunication Services in the Manufacturing Industry." *Information Economics and Policy* 4 (1) (1989-1990): 45-55.

———, ed. *The Economics of Information Networks.* Amsterdam: North-Holland, 1992.

Ardis, Susan, and Karen S. Croneis. "Document Delivery, Cost Containment and Serial Ownership." *College & Research Libraries News* 10 (November 1987): 624.

Arrow, Kenneth J. "Limited Knowledge and Economic Analysis." *American Economic Review* 64, no. 1 (March 1974): 1-10.

———. "The Value and Demand for Information." In *Collected Papers of Kenneth J. Arrow: Volume 4: The Economics of Information,* edited by Kenneth J. Arrow. Cambridge, MA: Harvard University Press, 1984.

Babe, Robert E., ed. *Information and Communication in Economics.* Recent Economic Thought Series. Boston: Kluwer Academic, 1994.

Baumol, William J., and Janusz A. Ordover. "Public Good Properties in Reality: The Case of Scientific Journals." In *Information Politics: Proceedings of the American Society for Information Science Annual Meeting,* edited by Susan K. Martin. Washington, DC: ASIS, 1976.

Baumol, William J., and Yale M. Braunstein. "Empirical Study of Scale Economies and Production Complementarity: The Case of Journal Publication." *Journal of Political Economy* 85, no. 5 (October 1977): 1037-48.

Bebensee, Mark, Bruce Strauch, and Katina Strauch. "Elasticity and Journal Pricing." *The Acquisitions Librarian* (1989): 219-28.

Becker, Gary S. *Economic Theory.* New York: Knopf, 1971.

———. *A Treatise on the Family.* Cambridge, MA: Harvard University Press, 1991.

Berg, Sanford V. "Copyright, Conflict, and a Theory of Property Rights." *Journal of Economic Issues* 5, no. 2 (June 1971): 71-79.

Besen, Stanley M. "Private Copying, Reproduction Costs, and the Supply of Intellectual Property." *Information Economics and Policy* 2, no. 1 (1986): 5-22.

———. "The Value of Television Time." *Southern Economic Journal* 42, no. 3 (January 1976): 435-41.

———. "The Value of Television Time: Some Problems and Attempted Solutions: Reply." *Southern Economic Journal* 44, no. 4 (April 1978): 1016-18.

Besen, Stanley M., and Leo J. Raskind. "An Introduction to the Law and Economics of Intellectual Property." *Journal of Economic Perspectives* 5, no. 5 (Winter 1991): 3-28.

Besen, Stanley M., and Sheila Nataraj Kirby. "Private Copying, Appropriability, and Optimal Copying Royalties." *Journal of Law and Economics* 32, no. 2 (October 1989): 255-80.

Besen, Stanley M., Willard G. Manning Jr., and Bridger M. Mitchell. "Copyright Liability for Cable Television: Compulsory Licensing and the Case Theorem." *Journal of Law and Economics* 21(1) (April 1978): 67-95.

Bester, Helmut. "Screening vs. Rationing in Credit Markets with Imperfect Information." *American Economic Review* 75, no. 4 (September 1985): 850-55.

Bickner, Robert E. "Concepts of Economic Cost." In *Cost Considerations in Systems Analysis*, edited by Gene H. Fisher, 24-63. New York: American Elsevier Publishing Company, 1971.

Biddle, Jeff E., and Daniel S. Hamermesh. "Sleep and the Allocation of Time." *Journal of Political Economy* 98, no. 5, part 1 (October 1990): 922-43.

Bittlingmayer, George. "The Elasticity of Demand for Books, Resale Price Maintenance and the Lerner Index." *Journal of Institutional and Theoretical Economics* 148, no. 4 (1992): 588-606.

Bloch, Harry, and Michael Wirth. "The Demand for Pay Services on Cable Television." *Information Economics and Policy* 1, no. 4 (1984): 311-32.

Bonk, Sharon C., and Dennis Pilling. "Modelling the Economics of Interlending." *Interlending & Document Supply* 18 (April 1990): 52-56.

Bookstein, Abraham. "An Economic Model of Library Service." *Library Quarterly* 51, no. 4 (1981): 410-28.

Braunstein, Yale M. "Costs and Benefits of Library Information: The User Point of View." *Library Trends* 28, no. 1 (Summer 1979): 79-87.

———. "Information as a Commodity: Public Policy Issues and Recent Research." In *Information Services: Economics, Management, and Technology*, edited by R. M. Mason and J. E. Creps, 9-22. Boulder, CO: Westview Press, 1981.

———. "Resolving Conflicts Between Information Ownership and Intellectual Freedom." *Library Trends* 39 (Summer-Fall 1990): 126-31.

Breyer, Stephen. "The Uneasy Case for Copyright: A Study of Copyright in Books, Photocopies, and Computer Programs." *Harvard Law Review* 84 (December 1970): 281-351.

Brockman, John R. *The Costs of Academic Libraries: An Econometric Interpretation.* Perth, Australia: Library of Curtain University of Technology, 1988.

Budd, John M. "It's Not the Principle, It's the Money of the Thing." *Journal of Academic Librarianship* 15, no. 4 (1989): 218-22.

Byrd, Gary D. "An Economic 'Commons' Tragedy for Research Libraries: Scholarly Journal Publishing and Pricing Trends." *College & Research Libraries* 51, no. 3 (1990): 184-95.

Casper, Cheryl. "Estimating the Demand for Library Services: Theory and Practice." *Journal of the American Society for Information Science* 29, no. 5 (September 1978): 232-37.

Chressanthis, George A. "The Cost Structure and Benefit Impact of Academic Libraries at American Research Universities." In *Economics of Information: Conference Proceedings*. Lyon, France: ENSSIB, 1995.

Chressanthis, George A., and June D. Chressanthis. "A General Econometric Model of the Determinants of Library Subscription Prices and Scholarly Journals: The Role of Exchange Rate Risk and Other Factors." *The Library Quarterly* 64 (1994): 270-93.

———. "Publisher Monopoly Power and Third-Degree Price Discrimination of Scholarly Journals." *Technical Services Quarterly* 11, no. 2 (1993): 13-36.

———. "The Relationship Between Manuscripts Submission Fees and Journal Quality." *The Serials Librarian* 24, no. 1 (1993): 71-86.

Courville, Leon, and Warren H. Hausman. "Warranty Scope and Reliability Under Imperfect Information and Alternative Market Structures." *Journal of Business* 52, no. 3 (July 1979): 361-78.

Crandall, R. W. "Elasticity of Demand for Cable Service and the Effect of Broadcast Signals on Cable Prices." Appended to TCI Reply Comments in FCC Mass Media Docket, 1990, 90-94.

Cronin, Blaise, and Elisabeth Davenport. *Elements of Information Management.* Metuchen, NJ: Scarecrow Press, 1991.

Cronin, Francis J., et al. "Telecommunications and Cost Savings in Health Care Services." *Southern Economic Journal* 61, no. 2 (1994): 343-55.

Cummings, Anthony M., Marcia L. Witte, William G. Bowen, Laura O. Lazarus, and Richard H. Ekman. *University Libraries and Scholarly Communications.* (Washington, DC: Association of Research Libraries for the Andrew W. Mellon Foundation, 1992).

Cummings, Martin M. "Cost Analysis: Methods and Realities." *Library Administration & Management* 3 (Fall 1989): 181-83.

———. *The Economics of Research Libraries.* Washington, DC: Council on Library Resources, 1986.

Daly, George, and Thomas Mayor. "Estimating the Value of a Missing Market: The Economics of Directory Assistance." *Journal of Law and Economics* 23, no. 1 (1980): 147-66.

Deacon, Robert T., and Jon Sonstelie. "Rationing by Waiting and the Value of Time: Results from a Natural Experiment." *Journal of Political Economy* 93, no. 4 (August 1985): 627-47.

DeBoer, Larry. "Economies of Scale and Input Substitution in Public Libraries." *Journal of Urban Economics* 32, no. 2 (September 1992): 257-68.

de Groot, Hans, Walter McMahon, and Fredericks J. Volkwein. "The Cost Structure of American Research Universities." *Review of Economics and Statistics* 73, no. 3 (1991): 424-31.

Demsetz, Harold. "Information and Efficiency: Another Viewpoint." *The Journal of Law and Economics* (1969): 1-22.

Diamond, Peter, and Michael Rothschild, eds. *Uncertainty in Economics: Readings and Exercises.* Revised edition. Economic Theory, Econometrics, and Mathematical Economics Series. San Diego: Harcourt Brace Jovanovich, 1989.

Doessel, D. P. "Medical Diagnosis as a Problem in the Economics of Information." *Information Economics and Policy* 2, no. 1 (1986): 49-68.

Eagly, Robert V. "Economics Journals as a Communications Network." *Journal of Economic Literature* 13, no. 3 (September 1975): 878-88.

Englund, Steven R. "Idea, Process, or Protected Expression?: Determining the Scope of Copyright Protection of the Structure of Computer Programs." *Michigan Law Review* 88 (February 1990): 866-909.

Fry, Bernard, and Herbert S. White. *Publishers and Libraries: A Study of Scholarly and Research Journals.* Lexington, MA: D. C. Heath and Company, 1976.

Galatin, Malcolm, and Robert D. Leiter, eds. *Economics of Information.* Boston: Martinus Nijhoff Publishing, 1981.

Galvin, Thomas J., and Allen Kent, eds. *Library Resource Sharing.* New York: Marcel Dekker, 1977.

Getz, Malcolm. "Depository Libraries and the Economics of Electronic Information." *The Bottom Line* 1, no. 3 (1987): 39-40.

———. "Economics: Document Delivery." *The Bottom Line* 5 (Winter 1991-1992): 40-44.

———. "Economics: Electronic Information; Storage, Communication, and Access." *The Bottom Line* 2, no. 3 (1988): 39-40.

———. "Economics: How Journals Are Priced." *The Bottom Line* 2, no. 4 (1988): 37-39.

———. "Economics: Increasing the Value of User Time." *The Bottom Line* 1, no. 2 (1987): 37-39.

———. "Economics: Pricing Photocopies." *The Bottom Line* 1, no. 1 (1987): 43-45.

———. "Electronic Publishing: An Economic View." *Serials Review* 18, nos. 1-2 (1992): 25-31.

———. "More Benefits of Automation." *College & Research Libraries* 49, no. 6 (November 1988): 534-44.

———. *Public Libraries: An Economic View.* Baltimore: Johns Hopkins University Press, 1980.

———. "Some Benefits of the Online Catalog." *College & Research Libraries* 48, no. 3 (May 1987): 224-40.

Giacoma, Pete. *The Fee or Free Decision; Legal, Economic, Political, and Ethical Perspectives for Public Libraries.* New York: Neal-Schuman Publishers, 1989.

Goldberg, Victor P. "The Economics of Product Safety and Imperfect Information." *Bell Journal of Economics* 5, no. 2 (Autumn 1974): 683-88.

Greenwald, Bruce C., and Joseph E. Stiglitz. "Externalities in Economies with Imperfect Information and Incomplete Markets." *Quarterly Journal of Economics* 101, no. 2 (May 1986): 229-64.

Griffiths, Jose-Marie, and Donald W. King. *Special Libraries: Increasing the Information Edge.* Washington, DC: Special Libraries Association, 1993.

Grossman, Sanford. "The Informational Role of Warranties and Private Disclosure About Product Quality." *Journal of Law and Economics* 24, no. 3 (December 1981): 461-83.

Grycz, Czeslaw Jan. "Economic Models for Networked Information." *Serials Review* 18, nos. 1-2 (1992): 11-18.

Haley, Jean Walstrom, and James Talaga. "Academic Library Responses to Journal Price Discrimination." *College & Research Libraries* 53 (January 1992): 61-70.

———. "Marketing Theory Applied to Price Discrimination in Journals." *The Journal of Academic Librarianship* 16, no. 6 (1991): 348-50.

Hall, Kent. "The Economic Nature of Information." *The Information Society* 1, no. 2 (1981): 143-66.

Harris, Matthew R. "Copyright, Computer Software, and Work Made for Hire." *Michigan Law Review* 89, no. 3 (December 1990): 661-701.

Helpman, Elhanan. "Innovation, Imitation, and Intellectual Property Rights." *Econometrica* 61, no. 6 (November 1993): 1247-80.

Holtmann, A. G., T. Tabasz, and W. Kruse. "The Demand for Local Public Services, Spillovers, and Urban Decay: The Case of Public Libraries." *Public Finance Quarterly* 4, no. 1 (January 1976): 97-113.

Iannaccone, Laurence R. "The Consequences of Religious Market Structure: Adam Smith and the Economics of Religion." University of Western Ontario Papers in Political Economy Report, 1991.

———. "Sacrifice and Stigma: Reducing Free-Riding in Cults, Communes, and Other Collectives." *Journal of Political Economy* 100, no. 2 (1992): 271-91.

Jackson, Mary E. "Library to Library: Fitting the Bill." *Wilson Library Bulletin* 66, no. 10 (June 1992): 95-97.

Johansson, J. K., and Arieh Goldman. "Income, Search, and the Economics of Information Theory: An Empirical Analysis." *Applied Economics* 11, no. 4 (December 1979): 435-49.

Johnson, William R. "The Economics of Copying." *Journal of Political Economy* 93, no. 1 (February 1985): 158-74.

Jordan, J. S. "The Economics of Accounting Information Systems." *American Economic Review* 79, no. 2 (May 1989): 140-45.

Jorgenson, D. W., and K. Yun. "The Excess Burden of Taxation in the U.S." Harvard Institute for Economic Research, Discussion Paper 1528, 1990.

Jowett, Paul, and Margaret Rothwell. *The Economics of Information Technology.* New York: St. Martin's Press, 1986.

Joyce, Patrick. "Price Discrimination in 'Top' Scientific Journals." *Applied Economics* 22, no. 8 (August 1990): 1127-35.

Kantor, Paul B. "Library Cost Analysis." *Library Trends* 38, no. 2 (Fall 1989): 171-88.

———. "Three Studies of the Economics of Academic Libraries." *Advances in Library Administration and Organization* 5 (1986): 221-86. JAI Press.

Kay, John. "The Economics of Intellectual Property Rights." *International Review of Law and Economics* 13, no. 4 (December 1993): 337-48.

Kenkel, James L. "The Economics of Information and Search for Prices and Wages." *Journal of Economics and Business* 27, no. 3 (Spring 1975): 209-18.

King, Donald W. "Pricing Policies in Academic Libraries." *Library Trends* 28, no. 1 (1979): 47-62.

Kingma, Bruce R. "Access to Journal Articles: An Economic Model of Document Delivery and Library Resource Sharing." *American Society for Information Science Conference Proceedings* 30 (1994): 8-16.

——. "An Accurate Measurement of the Crowd-Out Effect, Income Effect, and Price Effect for Charitable Contributions." *Journal of Political Economy* 95, no. 5 (1989): 1197-1207.

——. "The Demand for Photocopies and Journal Subscriptions: An Empirical Test of the Librarians' Solution to Journal Pricing." unpublished manuscript, School of Information Science and Policy, State University of New York at Albany, 1994.

Kingma, Bruce R., and Philip B. Eppard. "Journal Price Escalation and the Market for Information: The Librarians' Solution." *College & Research Libraries* 53 (November 1992): 523-35.

Klein, Lewis. "The Cost Effectiveness of Science Journals." *Publishing Research Quarterly* 8, no. 3 (1992): 72-91.

Koenig, Michael E. D., and Johanna Goforth. "Libraries and the Cost Recovery Imperative." *IFLA Journal* (1993): 261-79.

Kraft, Donald H., and Bert R. Boyce. *Operations Research for Libraries and Information Agencies: Techniques for the Evaluation of Management Decision Alternatives.* San Diego: Academic Press, 1991.

Kutz, Myer. "Distributing the Costs of Scholarly Journals: Should Readers Contribute?" *Serials Review* 18, nos. 1-2 (1992): 73-74.

Kurzweil, Raymond. "The Economics of Innovation." *Library Journal* 116, no. 17 (October 15, 1991): 54.

Lamberton, Donald M. "Cyberspace Economics." *Australian and New Zealand Journal of Serials Librarianship* 3, no. 2 (1992): 89-94.

——. "The Economics of Information and Organization." *Annual Review of Information Science and Technology* 19 (1984): 3-30.

——. "Research Development in the Economics of Information." *American Society for Information Science. Management of Information Systems: Proceedings.* White Plains, NY: Knowledge Industry. 1978.

Landes, William M., and Richard A. Posner. "An Economic Analysis of Copyright Law." *Journal of Legal Studies* 18, no. 2 (June 1989): 325-63.

Lankford, Hamilton. "Preferences of Citizens for Public Expenditures on Elementary and Secondary Education." *Journal of Econometrics* 27, no. 1 (January 1985): 1-20.

Leffler, Keith B., "Persuasion or Information? The Economics of Prescription Drug Advertising." *Journal of Law and Economics* 24, no. 1 (April 1981): 45-74.

Lewis, David W. "Economics of the Scholarly Journal." *College & Research Libraries* 50, no. 6 (November 1989): 674-88.

——. "Why Books Are Bought and Borrowed." *The Bottom Line* 2, no. 4 (1988): 21-24.

Liebowitz, Stanley J. "Copying and Indirect Appropriability: Photocopying of Journals." *Journal of Political Economy* 93, no. 5 (October 1985): 945-57.

——. "The Impact of Reprography on the Copyright System," report for the Bureau of Consumer and Corporate Affairs of Canada, 1981.

Liebowitz, Stanley J., and Stephen E. Margolis. "Journals as Shared Goods: Comment." *American Economic Review* 72, no. 3 (June 1982): 597-602.

Lippman, Steven A., and John J. McCall. "The Economics of Belated Information." *International Economic Review* 22, no. 1 (February 1981): 135-46.

Machlup, Fritz. "Publishing Scholarly Books and Journals: Is It Economically Viable?" *Journal of Political Economy* 85, no. 1 (February 1977): 217-25.

Marvel, Howard P. "The Economics of Information and Retail Gasoline Price Behavior: An Empirical Analysis." *Journal of Political Economy* 84, no. 5 (October 1976): 1033-60.

Maxfield, Myles, Jr. "Potential Impact of the Securities and Exchange Commission's EDGAR System on the Market for Securities Information." Washington, DC: Mathematica Policy Research, 1984.

McCain, Roger A. "Information as Property and as a Public Good: Perspectives from the Economic Theory of Property Rights." *The Library Quarterly* 58, no. 3 (July 1988): 265-82.

McKenzie, Richard B. "The Economist's Paradigm." *Library Trends* 28, no. 1 (Summer 1979): 7-24.

Mincer, Jacob. *Schooling, Experience, and Earnings.* New York: Columbia University Press, 1974.

Moss, Laurence. "The Chicago Intellectual Property Rights Tradition and the Reconciliation of Coase and Hayek." *Eastern Economic Journal* 17, no. 2 (April-June 1991): 145-56.

Nelson, Jon P. "Accessibility and the Value of Time in Commuting." *Southern Economic Journal* 43, no. 3 (January 1977): 1321-29.

Nimmer, R. T., and P. A. Krauthaus. "Information as a Commodity: New Imperatives of Commercial Law." *Law and Contemporary Problems* 55, no. 3 (Summer 1992): 103-30.

Noll, Roger, and W. Edward Steinmueller. "An Economic Analysis of Scientific Journal Prices: Preliminary Results." *Serials Review* 18, nos. 1-2 (1992): 32-37.

Novos, Ian E., and Michael Waldman. "The Emergence of Copying Technologies: What Have We Learned?" *Contemporary Policy Issues* 5, no. 3 (July 1987): 34-43.

Odagiri, Hiroyuki. "Demand for Economics Journals: A Cross Section Analysis." *Review of Economics and Statistics* 59, no. 4 (November 1977): 493-99.

O'Hare, Michael. "Copyright: When Is Monopoly Efficient?" *Journal of Policy Analysis and Management* 4, no. 3 (Spring 1985): 407-18.

Okerson, Ann. "With Feathers: Effects of Copyright and Ownership on Scholarly Publishing." *College & Research Libraries* 52, no. 5 (1990): 111-19.

Ordover, Janusz A., and Robert D. Willig. "Journals as Shared Goods: Reply." *American Economic Review* 72, no. 3 (June 1982): 603-7.

———. "On the Optimal Provision of Journals qua Sometimes Shared Goods." *American Economic Review* 63, no. 3 (June 1978): 324-38.

Palmer, John, ed. *The Economics of Patents and Copyrights.* Research in Law and Economics Series, vol. 8. Greenwich, CT: JAI Press, 1986.

Palmour, Vernon E., Marcia C. Bellassai, and Robert R. V. Wiederkehr. *Costs of Owning, Borrowing, and Disposing of Periodical Publications.* Arlington, VA: Center for Naval Analysis, 1977.

Park, Rolla Edward. "The Value of Television Time: Some Problems and Attempted Solutions: Comment." *Southern Economic Journal* 44, no. 4 (April 1978): 1006-15.

Peters, Elizabeth. "Marriage and Divorce: Informational Constraints and Private Contracting." *American Economic Review* (1986): 237-54.

Petersen, H. Craig. "The Economics of Economics Journals: A Statistical Analysis of Pricing Practices by Publishers." *College & Research Libraries* 53, no. 2 (March 1992): 176-81.

Peyton, David. "A New View of Copyright." *Journal of Policy Analysis and Management* 6, no. 1 (Fall 1986): 92-98.

Ramsey, Frank P. "A Contribution to the Theory of Taxation." *Economic Journal* 37 (March 1927): 47-61.

Reinganum, Jennifer F. "Technology Adoption Under Imperfect Information." *Bell Journal of Economics* 14, no. 1 (Spring 1983): 57-69.

Repo, Aatto J. "Economics of Information." *Annual Review of Information Science and Technology* 22 (1987): 3-35.

———. "The Value of Information: Approaches in Economics, Accounting, and Management Science." *Journal of the American Society for Information Science* 40, no. 2 (March 1989): 68-85.

Roberts, Carla M. "Worthy of Rejection: Copyright as Community Property." *Yale Law Journal* 100, no. 4 (January 1991): 1053-72.

Rothschild, Michael, and Joseph E. Stiglitz. "Equilibrium in Competitive Insurance Markets: An Essay on the Economics of Imperfect Information." *Quarterly Journal of Economics* 90, no. 4 (November 1976): 630-49.

Rubin, Michael R. *Information Economics and Policy in the United States.* Littleton, CO: Libraries Unlimited, 1983.

Rubinovitz, Robert N. "Market Power and Price Increases for Basic Cable Service Since Deregulation." *Rand Journal of Economics* 24, no. 1 (1993): 1-18.

Saffady, William. "The Availability and Cost of Online Search Services." *Library Technology Reports* 28, no. 2 (March/April 1992): 115-268.

Samuelson, Paul A., and William D. Nordaus. *Economics*, 15th edition. New York: McGraw Hill, 1995.

Sappington, David E. M., and Joseph E. Stiglitz. "Privatization, Information and Incentives." *Journal of Policy Analysis and Management* 6, no. 4 (Summer 1987): 567-82.

Schauer, Bruce P. *The Economics of Managing Library Services*. Chicago: American Library Association, 1986.

Schwartz, Alan, and Louis L. Wilde. "Product Quality and Imperfect Information." *Review of Economic Studies* 52, no. 2 (April 1985): 251-62.

Schweser, Carl. "The Economics of Academic Publishing." *Journal of Economic Education* 14, no. 1 (Winter 1983): 60-64.

Silk, Alvin J., and Ernst R. Berndt. "Scale and Scope Effects on Advertising Agency Costs." *Marketing Science* 12, no. 1 (1993): 53-72.

Simpson, Donald B. "Library Consortia and Access to Information: Costs and Cost Justification." *Journal of Library Administration* 12, no. 3 (1990): 83-97.

Smith, Adam. *An Inquiry into the Nature and Causes of the Wealth of Nations*. Reprint of 1776 edition. New York: Oxford University Press.

Smith, G. Stevenson. *Managerial Accounting for Libraries and Other Not-for-Profit Organizations*. Chicago: American Library Association, 1991.

Spence, Michael. "An Economist's View of Information." In *Annual Review of Information Science and Technology*, vol. 9, edited by Carlos A. Cuadra and Ann W. Luke, 57-78. Washington, DC: American Soceity for Information Science. 1974.

———. "Job Market Signaling." *Quarterly Journal of Economics* 83, no. 3 (August 1973): 355-74.

———. "Television Programming, Monopolistic Competition, and Welfare." *Quarterly Journal of Economics* 91, no. 1 (1977): 103-26.

Stigler, George J. "The Economics of Information." *The Journal of Political Economy* (1961).

Stiglitz, Joseph E. "Information and Economic Analysis." *Economic Journal* 95, no. 0 (Supplement 1985): 21-41.

———. "Monopoly, Non-Linear Pricing and Imperfect Information: The Insurance Market." *Review of Economic Studies* 44, no. 3 (October 1977): 407-30.

Stoneman, Paul. "Copying Capabilities and Intertemporal Competition Between Joint Input Technologies: CD vs DAT." *Economics of Innovation and New Technology* 1, no. 3 (1991): 233-41.

Stoller, Michael A. "Economic Issues in Copying Easily Reproducible Goods." *Journal of Consumer Policy* 14, no. 4 (1991-1992): 393-411.

Van House, Nancy A. *Public Library User Fees: The Use and Finance of Public Libraries*. Westport, CT: Greenwood Press, 1983.

———. "Research on the Economics of Libraries." *Library Trends* 32, no. 4 (Spring 1984): 407-23.

Varian, Hal R., and Jeffrey K. Mackie-Mason. "Some Economics of the Internet." working paper 93-16, University of Michigan Center for Research on Economic and Social Theory, 1993.

Von Hayek, F. "The Use of Knowledge in Society." *American Economic Review* 35, no. 4 (September 1945).

Weech, Terry L. "The Economics of Information and the Professional Training of Librarians and Information Scientists in the United States." *Economics of Information: Conference Proceedings.* Lyon, France: ENSSIB: 1995.

———. "The Teaching of Economics of Information in Schools of Library and Information Science in the U.S.—A Preliminary Analysis." *American Society for Information Science Conference Proceedings* 30 (1994): 70-75.

Westland, J. C. "Congestion and Network Externalities in the Short Run Pricing of Information System Services." *Management Science* 38, no. 7 (July 1992): 992-1009.

Williamson, Robert W. "Presenting Information Economics to Students." *Accounting Review* 57, no. 2 (April 1982): 414-19.

Wilson, Paul W. "Scheduling Costs and the Value of Travel Time." *Urban Studies* 26, no. 3 (June 1989): 356-66.

Winter, Harold. "Sequential Torts with Imperfect Information." *International Review of Law and Economics* 14, no. 1 (March 1994): 35-40.

Wood, Sandra M., ed. *Cost Analysis, Cost Recovery, Marketing, and Fee-Based Services: A Guide for the Health Sciences Librarian.* New York: Haworth Press, 1985.

Woolsey, W. William, and A. Bruce Strauch. "The Impact of U.S. Dollar Depreciation on the Prices of Foreign Academic Journals: A Supply and Demand Analysis." *Publishing Research Quarterly* 8, no. 1 (Spring 1992): 74-81.

Young, Ralph. "An Exploratory Analysis of Demand for the Public Library Lending Service." *Applied Economics* 5, no. 2 (June 1973): 119-32.

Zahray, W. Paul, and Marvin Sirbu. "The Provision of Scholarly Journals by Libraries via Electronic Technologies: An Economic Analysis." *Information Economics and Policy* 4, no. 2 (1989-1990): 127-54.

Index

193